What Do Psychoanalysts Want?

Is analysis a therapy or is it a scientific procedure which may be incidentally therapeutic?

Defining the aims of psychoanalysis was not initially a serious conceptual problem. However, when Freud began to think of the aim as being one of scientific research, and added the different formulations of aim (for example, that the aim was to make the patient's unconscious conscious), it became an area of tension which affected the subsequent development of psychoanalysis, the resolution of which has profound implications for the future of psychoanalysis.

In *What Do Psychoanalysts Want?* the authors look at the way psychoanalysts on both sides of the Atlantic have defined analytic aims, decade by decade, from Freud to the present day. On this basis they develop a theory about aims which is extremely relevant to clinical practice today, in which they discuss the issues from the point of view of the conscious and unconscious processes in the psychoanalyst's mind.

Besides presenting a concise history of psychoanalysis which will be of interest to a wide audience, this book makes important points for any analyst concerned to research his or her own practice.

Joseph Sandler is Emeritus Professor of Psychoanalysis, University College, London, and **Anna Ursula Dreher** is a University Lecturer and a psychoanalyst in private practice, Frankfurt.

THE NEW LIBRARY OF PSYCHOANALYSIS

The New Library of Psychoanalysis was launched in 1987 in association with the Institute of Psycho-Analysis, London. Its purpose is to facilitate a greater and more widespread appreciation of what psychoanalysis is really about and to provide a forum for increasing mutual understanding between psychoanalysts and those working in other disciplines such as history, linguistics, literature, medicine, philosophy, psychology and the social sciences. It is intended that the titles selected for publication in the series should deepen and develop psychoanalytic thinking and technique, contribute to psychoanalysis from outside, or contribute to other disciplines from a psychoanalytical perspective.

The Institute, together with the British Psycho-Analytical Society, runs a low-fee psychoanalytic clinic, organizes lectures and scientific events concerned with psychoanalysis, publishes the *International Journal of Psycho-Analysis* and the *International Review of Psycho-Analysis* and runs the only training course in the UK in psychoanalysis leading to membership of the International Psychoanalytical Association – the body which preserves internationally agreed standards of training, of professional entry, and of professional ethics and practice for psychoanalysis as initiated and developed by Sigmund Freud. Distinguished members of the Institute have included Michael Balint, Wilfred Bion, Ronald Fairbairn, Anna Freud, Ernest Jones, Melanie Klein, John Rickman and Donald Winnicott.

Volumes 1–11 in the series have been prepared under the general editorship of David Tuckett, with Ronald Britton and Eglé Laufer as associate editors. Subsequent volumes are under the general editorship of Elizabeth Bott Spillius, with, from Volume 17, Donald Campbell, Michael Parsons, Rosine Jozef Perelberg and David Taylor as associate editors

ALSO IN THIS SERIES

To Anne-Marie and Joachim

NEW LIBRARY OF PSYCHOANALYSIS
24

General editor: Elizabeth Bott Spillius

What Do Psychoanalysts Want?

The Problem of Aims in Psychoanalytic Therapy

JOSEPH SANDLER
ANNA URSULA DREHER

Foreword by Arnold M. Cooper

London and New York

First published 1996
by Routledge
11 New Fetter Lane, London EC4P 4EE

Simultaneously published in the USA and Canada
by Routledge
29 West 35th Street, New York, NY 10001

© 1996 Joseph Sandler and Anna Ursula Dreher

Typeset in Bembo by LaserScript, Mitcham, Surrey
Printed and bound in Great Britain by
Mackays of Chatham PLC, Chatham, Kent

British Library Cataloguing in Publication Data
A catalogue record for this book is available from the British Library

Library of Congress Cataloguing in Publication Data
A catalogue record for this book has been requested

ISBN 0–415–13514–1
ISBN 0–415–13515–X (pbk)

Contents

Foreword

ARNOLD M. COOPER

It takes persons of great courage, a quality that Sandler and Dreher seem to have in abundance, to write a book on 'What do psychoanalysts want?' The paraphrase on Freud's famous question carries with it the implication that analysts, at least in some aspects of their work, have been as confused, confusing and unknowable as Freud once thought women were. Of course, what was a reasonable mystery for the younger Freud who was in the process of creating psychoanalysis is today evidence of his gender bias. Similarly, Sandler and Dreher imply that now is an appropriate time to come to grips with some of the ambiguities, obscurities and vagueness that have characterised aspects of our thinking about and doing psychoanalysis, and to shed as much light on the question of what do analysts want as has been cast on that earlier question during the past near century. An underlying assumption of this exciting and challenging book is that knowing more about how our thinking has developed, clarifying the original implications and intentions of our ideas and tracing how they have changed over time in the course of competition with other ideas will help us to sort out what it is that we think, why we think as we do, and whether that is really how we want to think. It is consonant with Sandler's previous research on analysts' working theories to hold the view that analysts may have quite differing conscious and unconscious ideas of what they want, at times quite unaware of, and perhaps even disavowing, the working model that guides their work. Sandler and Dreher take the view that it can't hurt to try to be articulate about our thinking, and in writing this book they offer us the means to do better than we have done in the past in explicating our ideas of what it is that we are trying to achieve when we do analysis. Clearly, one aim of this volume is to help us to understand how in fact we are going about our analytic work. Interestingly, the question is put in terms of 'What do analysts want?' – not 'What do patients want?' It is a merit of this work that the intriguing title is only mildly facetious and the question it raises is more than justified by the extraordinary richness and depth of the answers that are provided. However, I cannot resist noting that it is hard to imagine any other branch of the healing arts asking 'What do the practitioners want?' – usually quite self-evident – or even asking 'What do patients want?' – which is usually equally self-evident.

The subtitle, 'The problem of aims in psychoanalytic therapy', poses the provocatively simple question: why do we and our patients engage in this complex, time-consuming, arduous and usually expensive enterprise? This exploration of aims provides the authors with the opportunity for an in-depth examination of the essential ingredients of the complex enterprise of psychoanalysis, and of how analysts' views on what we are doing have changed during the past century. Of course, the title assumes that there is an aim to this activity, giving short shrift to those who might maintain that analysis is aimless, a position that perhaps no one explicitly espouses, but which is close to the views of those who have maintained the circular proposition that the aim of psychoanalysis is to analyse, eschewing specific theoretical research, therapeutic or other 'practical' goals. In the effort to elucidate the aims of psychoanalysis, Sandler and Dreher have written a short but rather monumental account of the history of psychoanalytic aims, which, perhaps not surprisingly, turns out to be a history of psychoanalysis itself. This unique vantage point – i.e., the examination of our aims – provides the authors with the opportunity to concentrate on what most readers will find to be the heart of psychoanalytic history: those informing ideas that guide all our clinical activities, cutting through the details of how we conduct an analysis in order to achieve those aims. The great interest of psychoanalysts in technique, important in its own right, has sometimes obscured the obvious fact that technique is a means and not an end.

In the course of their investigations, the authors present brilliant summaries of the crux of the ideas of major movers of the field after Freud: Klein, Strachey, Fairbairn, Loewald, Kohut, Kernberg and others. Freed of any obligation to take cognizance of the politics or personalities of those involved, the authors concentrate on those analytic ideas that have changed the way analysts conceive and conduct their professional tasks. I know no comparable source for such wonderfully lucid, jargon-free descriptions of the thinking of our major innovators and what they have added to our psychoanalytic endeavour. In an era of theoretical pluralism, with clashing and competing ideas, this book serves an extremely important unifying function. Analysis, if it is a single activity, ought to have a reasonably unified set of aims that should cut across technical or theoretical differences within the discipline. When aims are not shared, it begins to be difficult to recognise the unity of the discipline that provides the foundation for a variety of applications.

Clearly, every new idea or claim for a change of analytic theory or technique has asserted that it is worthy of consideration on the grounds that it will be more successful in attaining some goal of the analyst's work than was the previous theory or technique. It would seem self-evident that any new theory or technique that did not make some kind of a detectable difference in the analytic work and its outcome would justifiably be deemed trivial and not worth serious study. The authors of this book do an admirable job of guiding us through the tangled thickets of competing analytic ideas, informing us how each idea contributed to a change in the analytic enterprise. Knowing the context in which ideas arose, and the currents that led to their modification, is enormously helpful in beginning to come to a better understanding of one's own experience and how we have come to hold the notions that inform our own psychoanalytic work.

This book is also particularly timely because in many parts of the psychoanalytic universe those who pay the bill – insurers and other varieties of third-party payers – are demanding an accounting of us. What do we achieve for our patient that justifies the cost? While certain of our justifiable analytic aims – for example increased self-knowledge or an enduring capacity for self-analysis – will never endear us to insurance companies, confusion and an avoidance of clarity concerning our aims and claims will surely damage us in other academic and research communities that are of great importance to us – medicine, for instance, or psychology, philosophy, literature and the arts. We are interested not only in resources to sustain patient treatment, but research funding and our standing in the intellectual community are also at stake.

The idea of presenting the story of the evolving aims of psychoanalysis in decade blocks provides a vivid panorama of the changing ideas of psychoanalysis, and a surprising sense of how rapidly and consistently we have been willing to change – sometimes without clear acknowledgement that we are doing so. Not only are we presented with a deep and penetrating review of Freud's changing concepts of the aims of analysis, but we are given a sense of Freud's willingness to see the aims of analysis differently according to his changing views of the structure of the mind and the analytic process. Freud was quite able to maintain differing and sometimes conflicting views of the aims of analysis without any apparent disturbance of his scientific equanimity. It is a fascinating story to see how one or another of Freud's multiple views became the sole or predominant view for later groups of analysts determined to bring about a unification of theory or see the predominance of a favourite point of view.

Each decade has been marked by one or more conflicts that centred that period's analytic discourse. These conflicts have included issues such as: therapeutic outcome aims versus psychoanalytic process aims; limited versus ambitious aims; relational versus intrapsychic aims, psychoanalysis viewed as a treatment versus psychoanalysis viewed as a research tool; outer-directed versus inner-directed criteria for change; clear therapeutic goals versus therapeutic neutrality; ideal or theoretical versus practical aims;

analysis as a limited versus an interminable process; primary aims of preserving the analytic process versus adopting a flexible (non-analytic?) stance to help the patient; the therapist as anonymous and neutral versus the therapist as participant and more or less self-revelatory. The list is expandable. There has been a gradual shift from the aim of symptom removal, to the attainment of insight, to the achievement of an internalised capacity for self-observation and self-analysis. A consistent issue underlying many of the specific disputes has been the discrepancy between the idealisation of the analytic method and the increasing recognition of limitations of the achievements of the method. This history of our aims shows us how these differing views have, with some exceptions, influenced one another, leading to new, more informed and sophisticated syntheses of how we understand analysis. The history of psychoanalysis includes intense battles and periodic attempts at reconciling disputes through some form of co-existence. We have been through periods of analytic hubris, when we thought we knew far more than we did and could achieve far more than we could, and we have alternated with probably more appropriate periods of analytic modesty and times of therapeutic pessimism.

The volume also provides us in passing with an account of the sociology of change in psychoanalysis. It is surprising to be reminded that it was not until the 1960s that we seriously began to see health in terms of flexible adaptation to life circumstances, including Aristotelian ideals of reasonableness and balance, and Sandler and Dreher remind us how significant cultural norms are in trying to understand any version of normality and its relation to the aims of psychoanalysis. Sandler and Dreher beautifully outline the continuing different perspectives on aims – historical-conceptual, socio-cultural and clinical-technical. It is also clear that there are always dual views of aims: the analyst's conscious and preconscious ideas of the overarching aims of psychoanalytic work, and the specific, and ever-changing, views of psychoanalytic aims that unfold during the interactions with each specific patient.

One of the many interesting discoveries in this book is the realisation of how enormous the changes in psychoanalysis have been. Even at its most 'orthodox', contemporary psychoanalysis has evolved and grown in directions that might not have been predicted even a few decades ago. The interest in research, including outcome studies, is growing, and even more important, the methodology for doing such research is improving. Professor Sandler has himself been a major contributor to the contemporary research ambience of psychoanalysis.

I am fully aware of the enormous contribution of Anna Ursula Dreher to this work. Without her wide knowledge of, and engagement in, conceptual research this book never would have been written. However, no introduction would be adequate without an acknowledgement of

Professor Sandler's very special role in the creation of contemporary psychoanalysis. In the interests of full disclosure, a sensitive issue here in the United States, I should reveal that Anne-Marie and Joe Sandler are dear personal friends of mine. I maintain that this only increases my capacity for assessing the true worth of Sandler's contributions to analysis. Joseph Sandler is that rare figure in the universe of psychoanalytic innovators whose work is characterised by a spirit of genuine exploration. He is willing to begin an examination of some significant aspect of psychoanalysis without a preconception of how the answer should come out. He has devoted much of his psychoanalytic life to exploring the taken-for-granted aspects of psychoanalysis – our standard concepts and ways of thinking and behaving psychoanalytically – and teasing out our fuzzy-mindedness and intellectual complacency, and our illogical and contradictory ideas. In a field that has been characterised by rather vigorous ideological disputes, he has shown the almost quaint capacity simultaneously to have complete faith in and dedication to psychoanalysis as a momentous intellectual, therapeutic and scientific activity, while being able to raise doubts concerning the validity of almost every analytic proposition – especially those that most of us take as self-evidently true. He has even been known to change his opinion on psychoanalytic issues. It is no contradiction for him to be a radical critic of our self-satisfaction, while maintaining a conservatism that leads him to preserve as much of the traditional and accepted ideas and ways of thinking as he can. He has introduced the idea of 'elasticity' of concepts to assist us in bringing our thinking into line with the requirements of logic and newer research, while not having to abandon totally ideas and terms with which we have long and loving relationships that would be too painful to terminate. With the advantage of being both a sophisticated clinician and an ingenious researcher, as well as an internationally known leader of our discipline and former president of the International Psychoanalytical Association, he has been instrumental in helping us to reformulate old ideas, and to conceive our new ones. Sandler has been one of the most creative figures in bringing about what I have termed a 'quiet revolution' in psychoanalytic theory during the past several decades. In a long series of extraordinary papers, one can observe the evolution of his thinking from the more traditional frame of reference with which he graduated from analytic training, towards the formation of a complex mixture of ego psychology and object-relations theory that has become the dominant frame of reference in much of today's psychoanalytic world, due in no small part to his work. While entirely courageous in following where his researches lead, he has never had a tendency to form a new school or to create new terminology.

This intellectual odyssey has been characterised by a consistent methodological effort to keep our theory tied to our clinical activity. His prior training as an experimental psychologist, statistically sophisticated and familiar with psychological tests and rating scales, enabled him to bring a fresh outlook to traditional concepts, supporting and altering these concepts on the basis of empirical research. He has been a bridging force in psychoanalysis, attempting to find the inherent linkages between apparently opposing ideas, and helping to close the gap between American ego psychologists, and British Kleinian and object-relations theorists.

Sandler has a long, perhaps unique, record of successful collaborations in his psychoanalytic work with many different co-authors. This volume with Anna Ursula Dreher is further evidence of how wonderfully fruitful such collaboration can be. This short and amazingly lucid history of psychoanalytic ideas challenges each of us to clarify how we think about psychoanalysis, as we enjoy this account of the great adventure of the development of psychoanalytic ideas. The encyclopaedic scope of this work seems incompatible with its brevity. I predict that this monograph will assume a place as a standard text in analytic institutes. I know no better way to orientate the student attempting to find his way among the now numerous major and minor points of view and frames of reference that demand allegiance as the better, truer, newer, or more classical or more orthodox version of psychoanalysis. Not the least of its virtues is that this book is a joy to read.

Preface

The topic dealt with in this book has, one way or another, received extensive attention in the psychoanalytic literature, but close examination of the concept reveals areas of unclarity and ambiguity. Difficulties even arise the moment one begins to consider terminology. The term 'aim' is used, on the whole, by British writers, whereas authors in the United States tend to write of 'goal'. Strictly speaking, the two terms have different though closely related meanings. Webster's dictionary (second edition) gives among its definitions of *aim* the following:

> to direct one's efforts; to attempt to reach or accomplish an object or purpose; to try or purpose to be or to do something.

The definition of *goal* includes:

> the end or final purpose; the end to which a design tends or which a person aims to reach or accomplish.

In German both aim and goal are rendered as *Ziel*. As a result, the choice of either aim or goal in the English translation of German psychoanalytic writings is made by the translator (as in the *Standard Edition* of Freud's works). Similarly in French the term *but* can be translated as both aim and goal. The same holds true for a number of other languages.

It is worth noting that some of the literature on psychotherapy outcome research distinguishes between aims or goals on the one hand, and objectives on the other. Webster defines an objective as 'something aimed at or striven for', i.e., it is a synonym for 'goal'. In practice, however, objectives are sometimes distinguished from goals or aims, in that the latter terms tend to be used in a more general sense, while objectives may be more specific and more operationally defined (e.g. an aim of therapy may be 'to improve the patient's mental health', as opposed to the objective of 'attaining greater success in work').

The psychoanalytic literature has tended not to take note of the distinction between aim and goal, and the two terms are for the most part used synonymously and interchangeably. The term 'objective' is not in common use. Because in this book we refer generously to the published literature in this area, we shall fall in, with some regret, with the general usage.

The text of this work contains a number of quotations, and we have taken the liberty of standardising the spelling throughout. Thus 'psychoanalysis' in a quotation is rendered as 'psychoanalysis', 'super-ego' as 'superego', 'fantasy' as 'phantasy', and so on. We hope that the licence we have given ourselves in this respect will not be offensive to the reader's eye. In order to be politically correct, yet to avoid having to say 'he and she', we spun a coin to determine which of the two we should use. On this basis we agreed to use 'he' and 'his' throughout.

Finally, we have tended to concentrate our efforts on reviewing the British and North American psychoanalytic literature, and we are aware that there have been significant publications on the topic in other countries. Nevertheless we believe that we have been able to assess the main issues relating to the problem of aims in psychoanalysis.

This book could not have been written without the support and critical assessments of a number of colleagues, foremost among whom are Arnold Cooper, Otto Kernberg, Riccardo Steiner, Robert Wallerstein and Daniel Widlöcher. Marion Burgner, Peter Goldberg, Anne-Marie Sandler, Stephen Seligman, Sally Weintrobe and Joachim Wutke made extremely useful suggestions. We are indebted to Paula Barkay, Martina Leber and Jane Pettit for their work on the manuscript. Above all, we are grateful to our editorial back-seat driver, Elizabeth Spillius, who patiently, persistently and untendentiously encouraged and advised us over the years in which we have been involved in this project. Finally, we acknowledge with gratitude the financial help provided for some of the expenses of this project by The Edith Ludowyk-Gyomroi Trust, London.

Joseph Sandler
Anna Ursula Dreher
London and Frankfurt,
March 1995

Introduction

When Freud first devised the psychoanalytic method as a method of therapy there was no ambiguity about the aims of the process. For both physician and patient the goal to be reached was that of 'healing' the patient. This meant that what was aimed for was the disappearance of the patient's symptoms as a result of an undoing or correction of the pathological processes which had led to the illness. Nevertheless, Freud was well aware that 'cure' could never be complete, and had, early in the history of psychoanalysis, responded to the question a hypothetical patient might put to him about how the method would help, by giving, albeit somewhat pessimistically, a clear statement of the way he saw the aim of psychoanalytic treatment: 'much will be gained if we succeed in transforming your hysterical misery into common unhappiness. With a mental life that has been restored to health you will be better armed against that unhappiness' (Freud, 1895, p. 305).

The problem of defining aims was not initially a serious conceptual one, as it was to become later when Freud began to think of the aim of analysis as being one of scientific research and added different formulations of aim (for example that the aim was to make the patient's unconscious conscious). As we shall see in the chapters that follow, changes in the way the aims of psychoanalysis were conceived reflected an important area of tension throughout the subsequent development of psychoanalysis, tension which was for the most part implicit and unrecognised, which persists to the present and revolves around the question: is analysis a therapy or is it a scientific procedure which has as its aim simply to analyse, but which may incidentally be therapeutic?

The answer to this question has profound implications for the future of psychoanalysis. Our own view, about which we came to be increasingly convinced during the course of writing this book, is that those who believe that the aim of the psychoanalytic method is no more and no less than to

1

analyse are deceiving themselves, and that all analysts are affected in their work by therapeutic aims, whether they know it or not. It will be seen that we regard as naive the frequently heard view that as analysts we do not have any other aim in our work with our patients than that of analysing. This view implies that the analyst is able to free himself completely of all therapeutic aims for the patient, keeping only to the goal of pursuing an 'uncontaminated' analysis.

A major source of difficulty in trying to clarify our understanding of aims has been the fact that proponents of different schools of analysis, working with psychoanalytic models which differ in important respects, present the aims of their therapeutic work in the light of their own theoretical orientations. With the growth and development of psycho-analysis, particularly since the Second World War, an increasing variety of different theoretical formulations has developed in the work of such groups of analysts as the ego psychologists, self psychologists, object-relations theorists, and members of the Kleinian school, and even within each of these groups different formulations of analytic aims have been put forward; aims such as working through the depressive position, increasing the cohesiveness of the self, giving greater autonomy to the ego, developing more concern for the object, and so on. These different theoretical viewpoints and emphases, with their different theoretical languages and metaphors, have contributed to the fact that the formulation of 'aim' or 'goal' has become incapable of being encompassed by a single simple for-mulation; its meaning is very dependent on the theoretical background of the author, and on the phase of the analytic process being considered. As Arnold Cooper puts it (1985), 'Our psychoanalytic literature has main-tained that there is a close relationship between psychoanalytic theory and psychoanalytic practice. However, since psychoanalytic theory has often been elaborated at high levels of abstraction, that unity of theory and practice may not always be as clear as we would wish. Theories that lack significant consequences for clinical work may be interesting for other purposes, but clearly cannot be held to be clinically valuable' (p. 5). From another angle, Riccardo Steiner (1994) points out, in discussing the prob-lems of communication between analysts who hold different theories, that many of these problems 'are due simply to the often naive ignorance with which we use extra-analytical assumptions, inevitably and constantly present in our work'. These assumptions 'are linked to various fields of knowledge and even to the socio-political milieu in which we live and above all, *to the specific moment in time of our personal development, and that of psychoanalysis and its context*' (p. 4). Yet it is striking that analysts who may be very far apart in the way they formulate their theoretical statements are much less apart when they come to clinical understanding and their

2

psychoanalytic practice. It is precisely this that led us to realise that the answer to the problem of aims was to be found in the processes that occur in the analyst's mind during the course of clinical psychoanalytic work. We shall discuss our conclusions about this in Chapter 9, but a few preliminary remarks may be useful at this point.

It can be said that the theories analysts use during the course of their work are of two sorts. The first are those theoretical statements that are readily accessible to the analyst's awareness. These have been referred to as *explicit* theories, usually 'official' theories with which the analyst feels identified and is comfortable with. The second category of theories is *implicit*, in that they have been created outside the analyst's consciousness during the course of analytic work and in the context of that work. Implicit theories play an important part in determining the course of an analysis. So, while there is no doubt that the analyst inevitably perceives and conceives the patient's material and the course of an analysis in terms of his own consciously available theory, his *unconscious* (strictly speaking, preconscious, i.e., unconscious in a descriptive sense) theories are, to say the least, equally important. Such theories can be prevented from reaching the analyst's awareness by repression or 'censorship' (Freud's so-called 'second censorship', operating just below the level of consciousness). Such unconscious theories 'are very much partial theories, models or schemata, which have the quality of being available in reserve, so to speak, to be called upon whenever necessary. That they may contradict one another is no problem. They coexist happily as long as they are unconscious' (Sandler, 1983, p. 38). It follows from this that while the analyst may consciously hold very definite theoretical views about the aims of analysis, he will also have unconscious ideas about what can and should be achieved through the analytic process; and we cannot equate the two.

We mentioned earlier the observation that analysts with different theoretical orientations may be closer on the clinical level than they are in terms of their 'public' theories. It seems likely that this is due to the fact that their implicit theories may be closer in that they are much more pragmatic than analysts' explicit theories. Moreover, the 'public' theories represent 'group' or 'school' allegiances and identifications, and therefore, of necessity, overemphasise theoretical differences.

The psychoanalyst also carries with him very personal unconscious theories, models, plans, strategies, rules for action and culturally determined values and attitudes. All of these have been organised throughout his development, and have been profoundly influenced by his social environment from the very beginning. In this regard, the analyst does not differ from anyone else. In the analytic situation he is, of course, affected not only by these personal unconscious theories, values, and the like, but also by those countertransferences which represent specific reactions to specific qualities in the patient.[1] Only some of his counter-transference reactions (using 'countertransference' in its broadest sense) will be accessible to him, but others will also be subject to the censorship mentioned earlier when speaking of implicit theories. There is no way in which the analyst can escape the influence of all these internal factors; moreover, there is no way in which he can be completely neutral in his contact with the patient. To a certain extent he may consciously control his subjective attitude, and it is a major part of his analytic task to try to be aware, as far as possible, of his own mental processes; but no matter how well analysed he may be, unconscious values and attitudes will exert their influence. Freud was, of course, well aware of this when he said, in 1923, that 'the normal man is not only far more immoral than he believes but also far more moral than he knows'(p. 52); and this applies not only to normal men but to psycho-analysts as well. In this context, Bion's recommendation that the analyst should enter each session free of memory and desire cannot be taken literally, and we do not think it was meant to be.

For many years it was advocated that analysts, in order to deal with personal biases that might interfere with their work with their patient, should adopt an attitude of neutrality in their work. Moore and Fine, in their *Psychoanalytic Terms and Concepts*, define neutrality as 'the stance of the analyst generally recommended for fostering the psychoanalytic process. Central to psychoanalytic neutrality are keeping the countertransference in check, avoiding the imposition of one's own values upon the patient, and taking the patient's capacities rather than one's own desires as a guide' (1990, p. 127). But they point to the 'increasing recognition that the analyst's values are always operative, especially those involving the search for truth, knowledge, and understanding, and those emphasising orien-

---

1 Sandler *et al.* (1992) suggest that 'a useful view of countertransference might be to take it as referring to the specific emotionally based responses aroused in the analyst by the specific qualities of his patient. This would exclude *general* features of, the analyst's personality and internal psychological structure (which would colour or affect his work with all his patients) and would imply (1) that there are countertransference responses in the analyst, and that these exist throughout the analysis; (2) that countertransference can lead to difficulties in, or inappropriate handling of, the analysis – this will occur if and when the analyst fails to become aware of aspects of his countertransference reactions to the patient, or fails to cope with them if he is aware of them; (3) that constant scrutiny by the analyst of variations in his feelings and attitudes towards the patient can lead to increased insight into processes occurring in the patient' (pp. 96–97).

tation toward reality, maturity and change. These attitudes affect the therapeutic process in complex ways' (ibid.).[2]

In this context 'neutrality' is an ideal condition which is impossible to reach. We cannot be completely neutral and survive in the world we live in, because survival involves continual, indeed moment-to-moment conscious and unconscious judgements based upon values we have attributed to different courses of action. Gardner Murphy, in his fascinating book on self-deception (1975) speaks of the way in which we acquire mental 'blinders' (blinkers) as well as 'selectors' when we learn to perceive and act upon the world around us. In order to survive 'there must be firm conviction that one sees the world as it really is . . . being imperfectly adapted to all of reality, [living things] must also accept much of the not-real as real. They must at times be self-deceived' (p. 4). And he says, 'We need magnifying glasses through which we can emphasise what seems good and . . . we need reversed opera glasses to reduce the size of a threat or a blow. We must accept the distortions that our needs require; we must accept the lenses that reduce the problems we cannot solve' (pp. 4–5). But, as Murphy points out, our 'blinders shut out evidence that would contribute to a balanced and objective view' (p. 5). However skilled an analyst may be, however neutral in his value judgements he may believe himself to be, blinkers and selectors will always be at work. So perhaps it is more appropriate to speak of conscious *control* rather than neutrality; but such control is limited and can only be exercised to the extent that the analyst is aware of the cognitive and emotional factors that affect his judgements.

We began this project on the assumption that the idea of the psychoanalytic treatment aim could be dealt with as if it were a concept which, following assessment, discussion and evaluation, could lead to the formulation of a coherent and plausible definition of what psychoanalysts mean when they refer to the aims or goals of their therapy. We originally planned to include a historical review of the field interspersed with reproductions of important and representative papers from the analytic literature, hoping that we could choose and comment on contributions which would lead us to relative precision in this area. After working on this project for some

---

2 Chessick, in *A Dictionary for Psychotherapists*, writes: 'Of course, neutrality also requires the analyst to be reasonably neutral with respect to religious, ethical, and social values; he or she must not direct the treatment according to some personal ideals and is expected not to read particular idiosyncratic meanings into the patient's free association according to his or her theoretical preconceptions. It is generally recognised that no therapist can be completely neutral, yet it is also agreed that neutrality is a most important goal for the therapist to strive to maintain' (1993, p. 258). The topic is also fully discussed by Schachter (1994).

time we were forced to the conclusion that this could provide neither us nor the reader with an encompassing formulation of the psychoanalytic concept of aims. We also realised that, in addition to papers specifically addressed to the topic, much was to be gained from an examination of analytic contributions which did not deal explicitly with it. Indeed, it became clear that crucial aspects of the ways in which aims are conceived are implicit in writings on such topics as the analytic process, indications for analysis, 'analysability', discussions of mental health, the concept of 'normality', criteria for termination of analysis, and in clinical descriptions of individual analyses. It was this that led us to the conclusion that precision about *the* aim of psychoanalysis was unattainable. Rather, we had to deal with multiple aims formulated by analysts who had different (at times very different) theoretical perspectives on the psychoanalytic method and the processes involved. So we decided not to reprint previously published papers in their original form, but have allowed ourselves to include a number of lengthy quotations.

In a way the process of creating this book can be compared to the analytic process itself. We started with the aim of, so to say, 'curing' the problem of aims by gaining insight into its underlying structure. During the course of the work, however, we found that we were heading towards conclusions which we had not anticipated, although these did not clarify themselves until we had more or less completed our review of the literature. And, as in the analytic patient's free associations, much of what we have written has a somewhat disconnected quality, but we would not enjoin the reader to follow Freud's recommendation to analysts to employ 'evenly suspended attention' in reading the literature review, as he would certainly find it extremely difficult. In spite of a degree of disconnectedness, our method of presentation and discussion of different points of view about aims has been a historical one, in which we have attempted to tease out the trends in psychoanalytic thinking in this area. In order to find a suitable way of ordering and presenting our material, consistent with a historical approach to the topic, we decided to present our review structured according to decades, beginning with the 1920s.

With the development of psychoanalysis during Freud's lifetime, more experience of the psychoanalytic method and greater clinical knowledge accumulated (Chapter 1). Increasing attention began to be paid to questions of psychoanalytic technique, to what were thought to be the effective agents in bringing about change in the patient. An important step was taken with the transition from Freud's topographical theory of the mind, as described in *The Interpretation of Dreams* (1900), with its major concepts of Unconscious, Preconscious and Perceptual-Conscious systems, to the so-called 'structural' theory, spelled out in *The Ego and the Id* (1923), and involving the mental agencies of id, ego and superego. With this transition, different conceptualisations of aim emerged, formulated for the most part in terms of desirable structural changes to be brought about by the application of the psychoanalytic method.[3] So, for example, the aim of bringing about modification of the patient's superego came to be given particular prominence in the psychoanalytic literature of the late 1920s and early 1930s (Chapter 2). Psychoanalysts were concerned to make the method as therapeutically effective as possible, at the same time being increasingly aware of its limitations. Issues of mental health and normality began to be considered, for example by Ernest Jones in 1931 and Heinz Hartmann in 1939 (Chapter 3). Changes in the psychoanalytic theory of the mind as well as in the technique of psychoanalysis profoundly influenced the formulation of aims, which in turn had repercussions on psychoanalytic theory and practice.

After the outbreak of the war in Europe in 1939, and in the immediate post-war period, the main centres of development in psychoanalysis were the United States and Britain (Chapter 4). In the United States training for psychoanalysis was almost entirely restricted to psychiatrists, and a number of training institutes were set up within medical schools. The link between psychoanalysis and psychiatry made it inevitable that the therapeutic effectiveness of psychoanalysis became a major concern of analysts and non-analysts alike, particularly as questions of the cost-effectiveness of psychoanalysis became more acute. All this increased the attention paid by psychoanalysts to questions of how therapeutic outcome could be evaluated. In fact the assessment of therapeutic outcome had interested psychoanalysts much before this, and both the Berlin Institute (Deutsche Psychoanalytische Gesellschaft, 1930) and the British Society (Glover, 1940) had undertaken statistical studies of analytic procedure and its effectiveness. In the United States, as early as 1941, Robert Knight had presented a paper on the evaluation of the results of psychoanalysis to a meeting of the American Psychiatric Association (Knight, 1942). A major symposium held at meetings of the Boston Psychoanalytic Society in 1948 was devoted to the same topic (Chapter 4). The need for and interest in 'outcome research' has increased in the United States and Europe over the years since and, with it, increased attention has been paid to the question of aims. In addition, formulations in this area have not always been put explicitly in terms of aims or goals, but have often been evident in

---

3 The idea of structural change refers to changes in what Merton Gill has called macrostructures (i.e., id, ego and superego considered as entities). Later conceptions of structural change tend to refer to microstructures (Gill, 1963), i.e., to smaller-scale enduring mental organisations, no matter how minute (e.g. perceptual or cognitive structures). Failure to distinguish between these two meanings of structure has been a frequent source of confusion.

7

discussions of outcome, termination of analysis and criteria for assessing therapeutic change.

Numerous other factors have operated to stimulate interest in the topic of aims, and have thrown light on the concept. Among these we can include issues of indications, prognosis and 'analysability', as these have come to the fore in the context of the application of psychoanalysis to conditions other than neurosis. This relates to the so-called 'widening scope' of psychoanalysis (Chapters 5 and 6), in which it was recognised that the psychoanalytic method was applicable to the treatment of delinquents, psychotics, cases of borderline personality disorder and narcissistic personality, as well as to people with other 'character' disorders. Of particular significance has been the widespread application of psychoanalytic theory and aspects of its technique to a whole variety of methods of therapy which differ from the psychoanalytic method but which have a claim to be 'psychoanalytic'. Indeed, the number of practitioners of psychoanalytic, psychodynamic and psychoanalytically orientated psychotherapy of different sorts now far exceeds the number of psychoanalysts (see Wallerstein, 1995). To the extent that such methods represent modifications of psychoanalytic technique, however appropriate and useful, they must also involve a modification of treatment aims, and the literature comparing psychoanalysis with psychotherapy is much concerned with differences in their respective aims.

Over the years many attempts have been made to clarify the issues. As early as 1934 Michael Balint, delivering a paper on 'The final goal of psychoanalytic therapy', distinguished between 'classical' and 'romantic' descriptions of the final goal of analysis. The 'classical' author considers aims in relation to structural changes in the mind, while the 'romantic' 'lays stress on the dynamic or the emotional factor' (1935, p. 190). The most comprehensive early enumeration of criteria which need to be considered in assessing the effectiveness of an analysis was presented by Knight, in the paper mentioned earlier. He includes, for example, as criteria of a satisfactory analytic outcome, improved interpersonal relationships and the gaining of sufficient insight to handle psychic conflicts and the stresses imposed by reality. In the years that followed, many authors addressed themselves, directly or indirectly, to specifying criteria along the same lines as Knight, at times from different theoretical backgrounds.

Interest in differentiating various 'levels' of aim began to be more apparent in the 1960s (Chapter 6). It was increasingly recognised that analyst and patient could have different aims, and that these aims could change during the course of an analysis. At this time we can also see a distinction between 'proximate' and 'distant' or 'ultimate' goals. Thus ultimate goals were said to be to help the patient to gain 'self-understanding, self-realisation and self-acceptance', while proximate goals are those immediately achievable in the psychoanalytic situation, and if achieved would enable the patient to gain knowledge of his unconscious motivation and emotions (Glueck, 1960). But in spite of significant further approaches to organising the concept of aims (Wallerstein, 1965; Ticho, 1972), problems remained in connection with the differentiation and integration of different psychoanalytic schools of thought (see Chapters 7 and 8).

As we have indicated, much of the literature relevant to aims will be spelled out in some detail in what follows. In the last chapter we shall put forward a schema for assessing and evaluating aims on the basis of three different perspectives, as they have been spelled out and contrasted in the analytic literature, from the point of view of the analytic work.

1 *The historical-conceptual perspective* includes the examination of aims from the point of view of the phases of theoretical development in psychoanalysis and the various 'schools' of psychoanalytic thought;

2 *the socio-cultural perspective* approaches aims from the point of view of mental health and normality within a particular societal context;

3 *the clinical and technical perspective* relates to distinctions between various types of analytic aim.

Finally, we have tried to give an outline of an approach to the topic, not a theory *of* aims, but rather a theory *about* aims, and to discuss some of the implications of such a theory. The issue of aims will be considered from the point of view of the conscious and unconscious processes occurring in the analyst's mind, and we shall put forward some suggestions for research in this area, hoping that this effort will clarify rather than confuse, for the present status of the psychoanalytic notion of aims of treatment is certainly one of relative confusion.

1

Freud's views on aims

Before devising the method of free association, Freud had made use of hypnosis and other techniques of suggestion in order to retrieve memories which he regarded as having been repressed as a consequence of trauma; but such methods were given up because he had found them to be therapeutically ineffective. These earlier forms of treatment had involved different attempts on the part of the physician, essentially based on suggestion, to force repressed memories into consciousness, with a resulting catharsis, a 'discharge' of affect; but the procedure of suggestion, Freud pointed out later, is like painting in which particles of colour are applied to the canvas – *per via di porre*, as Leonardo da Vinci had put it. Analytic therapy, as it was conceived by the turn of the century, proceeds, on the other hand, *per via di levare*, 'since it takes away from the block of stone all that hides the surface of the statue contained in it' (1905, p. 260).

In *The Interpretation of Dreams* (1900), Freud spelled out his 'topographical' theory of the mind, which involved a division of the 'mental apparatus' into the systems *Perceptual-Conscious, Preconscious* and *Unconscious*. The psychoanalytic 'cure' was not now achieved through catharsis, but rather by the interpretation of instinctual wishes and phantasies that had been repressed into the system Unconscious, and the conflicts with which they were associated. The approach to dream interpretation taken in 1900 had become the basis for the whole method of analysis. Ten years later, in speaking of a 'general effect' of psychoanalysis, Freud says, 'the psychoneuroses are substitutive satisfactions of some instincts the presence of which one is obliged to deny to oneself and others. Their capacity to exist depends on this distortion and lack of recognition. When the riddle they present is solved and the solution is accepted by the patients these diseases cease to be able to exist' (1910, p. 148). Freud's view at that time was that the illness was a disguised expression of the instinct (drive) so that the underlying wish was not recognised. This formulation paralleled his views about the formation of the dream as a concealed expression of an unconscious instinctual wish. The aim of the analytic method was to bring the 'latent' instinctual wish to consciousness and to overcome the resistance to its acceptance.[1]

It is important to note that Freud's orientation was consistently that of a physician and scientist, who had fully internalised the empirical approach and medical model of the late nineteenth century. Certainly there were many streams of influence, beside the scientific perspective of the time, that affected the development of Freud's thinking. He was in many ways a child of his time, affected by the changing attitudes towards late nineteenth-century Victorian values, by his mixed liberal and orthodox Jewish background, and by his enormous interest in literature and in philosophical ideas (see, for example, Jones, 1957; Gay, 1988; Ellenberger, 1970; Sulloway, 1979). But it was essentially his objectivist scientific approach that led him, in the course of developing the psychoanalytic method, to emphasise that it was not only a therapy but equally a method of research – a dual perspective reflected in his famous 'conjunction' statement that

> In psychoanalysis there has existed from the very first an inseparable bond between cure and research. Knowledge brought therapeutic success. It was impossible to treat a patient without learning something new; it was impossible to gain fresh insight without perceiving its beneficent results. Our analytic procedure is the only one in which this precious conjunction is assured. It is only by carrying on our analytic pastoral work that we can deepen our dawning comprehension of the human mind.
>
> (1927, p. 256)[2]

Freud gave equal weight to cure and research in the 'conjunction' statement of 1927, but there is evidence that the two aims were not in fact evenly balanced in his mind, and that this was a source of a conflict for analysts which remains to this day. Psychoanalytic research was the gaining of knowledge *through analysing*, and the problem of the 'aim to cure' as opposed to the aim to conduct research (that is, the aim to analyse) was, as

---

1 In the English editions of Freud's works the German *Trieb* was translated as 'instinct'. This is an unsatisfactory translation because Freud was not referring to 'instinctive' behaviour of the sort described by biologists. *Trieb* would be rendered more appropriately as 'drive', and indeed many psychoanalytic authors speak of 'the drives'. In order to maintain a connection with the original translation, the compromise terms 'instinctual drive' and 'instinctual wish' were introduced, and are now widely used.

2 Freud's double orientation towards cure and research was in fact present from early on. We can detect the link between therapy and research in his 1896 reference to 'the laborious but completely reliable method of psychoanalysis used by me in making those investigations which also constituted a therapeutic procedure' (1896, p. 162).

we shall see, to run like a thread through subsequent discussions of analytic aims, during Freud's lifetime and afterwards.

In 1909, Freud stated clearly that 'therapeutic success, however, is not our primary aim; we endeavour rather to enable the patient to obtain a conscious grasp of his unconscious wishes' (1909, p. 120). Implicit in this is Freud's view that the successful application of the psychoanalytic method would inevitably lead to beneficial therapeutic results in the patient. The analyst's task is to *analyse*, and if he is preoccupied with achieving a cure rather than confining himself to analysing the patient, this is inimical to the psychoanalytic process. Freud was quite outspoken in condemning the physician who was possessed by the *furor sanandi* – the passionate obsession to cure: 'As a doctor, one must above all be tolerant to the weakness of a patient, and must be content if one has won back some degree of capacity for work and enjoyment[3] for a person even of only moderate worth. Educative ambition is of as little use as therapeutic ambition' (1912, p. 119).

Freud was not entirely comfortable with the idea that the analytic method, strictly applied, should divest itself of therapeutic aims. In a paper entitled 'Recommendations to physicians practising psychoanalysis' (one of a series of writings on technique published between 1910 and 1915) he voiced concern about the antithetical properties of the therapeutic and research orientations. The aim of undertaking research on a patient's material during the analysis can, Freud said, interfere with the proper conduct of the treatment: 'One of the claims of psychoanalysis to distinction is, no doubt, that in its execution research and treatment coincide; nevertheless, after a certain point, the technique required for the one opposes that required for the other. It is not a good thing to work on a case scientifically while treatment is still proceeding' (1912, p. 114).

We have indicated that Freud must have experienced a conflict between his therapeutic aims, on the one hand, and the aims of research and the application of the psychoanalytic method, on the other. There was the natural wish of the physician to heal, yet there was the knowledge that a preoccupation on the part of the analyst with curing the patient of his ills could hinder the effectiveness of the analytic method. The way out of this dilemma was provided by the 'conjunction' notion and the belief that cure could only come about through the application of what Freud called 'strict

---

3 Freud has often been cited as having said that the aim of psychoanalytic therapy is to enable the patient to attain a greater capacity 'to work and to love'. We have been unable to trace this phrase in the *Standard Edition* of Freud's writings or in his *Gesammelte Werke*. However, Ilse Grubrich-Simitis has pointed out (personal communication) that she has never found this widely quoted phrase in Freud, except in a private context in two letters to his fiancée, made casually and '*absolutely not in regard to a treatment aim*'.

and untendentious psychoanalysis' (1919, p. 168). This approach to psycho-analytic therapy reflected a slight shift of emphasis in Freud's formulation of analytic aims which had been evident from early on. Less and less importance had been placed on the notion of 'cure', more on the *process* of analysis *per se* and on the aim of making what is unconscious conscious. In an article entitled 'Freud's psychoanalytic procedure' (1904) he had said,

> The task which the psychoanalytic method seeks to perform may be formulated in different ways, which are, however, in their essence equivalent. It may, for instance, be stated thus: the task of the treatment is to remove the amnesias. . . . Or the formula may be expressed in this fashion: all repressions must be undone. The mental condition is then the same as one in which all amnesias have been removed. Another formulation reaches further: the task consists in making the unconscious accessible to consciousness, which is done by overcoming the resistances.
>
> (1904, pp. 252–253)

Having stated the analytic task in this way, Freud nevertheless goes on to indicate his concern for the patient's recovery from his illness. So, a few lines further, we read that

> the aim of the treatment will never be anything else but the *practical* recovery of the patient, the restoration of his ability to lead an active life and of his capacity for enjoyment. In a treatment which is incomplete or in which success is not perfect, one may at any rate achieve a considerable improvement in the general mental condition, while the symptoms (though now of smaller importance to the patient) may continue to exist without stamping him as a sick man.
>
> (1904, p. 253)

The aim of making the unconscious conscious was not without obstacles. The analyst needs 'to recognise the *resistance* with which the patient clings to his disease and thus even fights against his own recovery; yet it is this phenomenon of resistance which alone makes it possible to understand his behaviour in daily life' (1905, p. 261). As Freud elaborated his theories of mental functioning (metapsychology), the idea of 'making the unconscious conscious' by overcoming the patient's resistance, as an aim of the method, was amplified. In 1906 he remarks: 'The aim of psychoanalysis is absolutely uniform in every case: complexes have to be uncovered which have been repressed because of feelings of unpleasure and which produce signs of resistance if an attempt is made to bring them into consciousness' (p. 112). Some years later Freud points out that the resistance 'accompanies the treatment step by step. Every single association, every act of the person under treatment must reckon with the resistance and represents a compromise between the forces that are striving towards recovery and the opposing ones . . .' (1912, p. 103).[4]

Interestingly, Freud's writings made much use of metaphors of this sort, which were based on a military model; inevitably these had a bearing on the ways in which the aims of psychoanalysis were conceived. Not only did the patient show 'resistance' and have to 'fight against his own recovery', but he experienced 'conflict', made use of 'defences', needed to be 'better armed against unhappiness', and so on. The idea that the patient has to fight against a sort of 'enemy within' seems to have influenced some psychoanalysts to see their work with their patients as a sort of battle in which the analyst has to fight with the enemy in the patient. In spite of the military metaphors, Freud was careful to avoid being tempted towards a moralistic criminalisation of the patient, but some of his followers have not managed to do this. Consequently Freud's liberal attitude towards such issues as homosexuality (Freud, 1935, p. 195–196) was not followed by those analysts who were determined to cure it in their patients (R. Steiner, personal communication).

The publication of the *Introductory Lectures on Psychoanalysis* (1916–17) marked an important step in Freud's thinking. The lectures were composed at a time when his theoretical views were undergoing significant development, as witnessed in his papers on narcissism (1914), on meta psychology (1915a, 1915b, 1915c) and in 'Mourning and melancholia' (1917). In his *Introductory Lectures* Freud provides the reader with an overview of psychoanalytic theory as he had developed it over two decades. In numerous comments on the aim of the method he amplified, restated, and in some instances modified many of his previous formulations.

Freud now takes the idea of making the unconscious conscious further, and notes that the outcome of this process is the transformation of the pathogenic conflict into a normal one 'for which it must be possible somehow to find a solution' (p. 435). He remarks that the patient, as a consequence of analysis,

> has rather less that is unconscious and rather more that is conscious in him than he had before. The fact is that [one is] . . . probably underestimating the importance of an internal change of this kind. The neurotic who is cured has really become another man, though at

---

[4] The patient's neurosis was seen as an outcome of conflict over infantile wishes and impulses, and these had been defended against. The analysis constituted an invitation to such wishes to express themselves, and because this intensified the patient's conflict, the patient resisted the effort of the analyst to bring them to the surface. Freud expanded on various other sources of resistance in *Inhibitions, Symptoms and Anxiety* (1926a).

bottom, of course, he has remained the same; that is to say, he has become what he might have become at best under the most favourable conditions . . . the ego was feeble, infantile, and may perhaps have had grounds for banning the demands of the libido as a danger. Today it has grown strong and experienced, and moreover has a helper at hand in the shape of the doctor. Thus we may expect to lead the revived conflict to a better outcome than that which ended in repression.

(1916–17, pp. 435, 438)

Although Freud had often insisted that the aim of psychoanalysis was to make the unconscious conscious, he went on to qualify this view in a way that had the greatest significance for the psychoanalytic method. He pointed out that the idea that translation by the analyst of what is unconscious can *by itself* bring about psychic change and result in cure is a shortsighted error. If the analyst simply conveys his understanding of what is unconscious to the patient, the new knowledge does not replace the unconscious material in the mind of the patient, but comes to exist beside it, with very little change resulting. So the analyst must look for the unconscious material in the patient's memory 'at the place where it became unconscious owing to a repression' (p. 436). What has become important is the removal of the *resistance* consequent on the repression, and this removal occurs by discovering the resistance and showing it to the patient. This resistance to conscious awareness was regarded by Freud as identical with one that took place earlier as a result of conflict, and the analyst now has to discover, understand and communicate it to the patient. Nevertheless he has to do it in the right place, and in his interpretations has to get back to the point in development at which the conflict arose. He has to work on the resistance which is now aroused because of the repetition of the unconscious conflictual wish in the present (particularly in the patient's relation to the analyst) and of the repression which has been directed against this wish.

An important conceptual step in the *Introductory Lectures* is the elaboration of Freud's idea of the transference neurosis. In the course of treatment 'we are no longer concerned with the patient's earlier illness but with a newly created and transformed neurosis which has taken the former's place' (p. 444). There is a transferring of the patient's essential neurotic conflict to the arena of the analysis, the analyst becoming the centre of the patient's preoccupations. It is a 'new edition of the old disorder', and the overcoming of this new and artificial (transference) neurosis coincides with cure. 'A person who has become normal and free from the operation of repressed instinctual impulses in his relation to the doctor will remain so in his own life after the doctor has once more withdrawn from it' (pp. 444–445). We can see, reflected in Freud's concern with the need for the development and overcoming of the transference neurosis, his concern with analysis as a procedure with therapeutic aims; and a central aim in this connection was the resolution of the neurotic conflict which had brought the patient to analysis.

It was clear that while Freud had retained the aim of analysis as being to make the unconscious conscious, in his *Introductory Lectures* he refined his views on what was necessary to achieve this aim. There he began to give more attention to the details of the *intrapsychic* alterations that occur in the patient as a consequence of analysis. This is evident in his comment that one cannot account for the therapeutic effect of psychoanalysis by its having made a full sexual life possible for the patient. Rather 'we accustom [the patients] . . . to giving unprejudiced consideration to sexual matters no less than to any others; and if, having grown independent after the completion of their treatment, they decide on their own judgement in favour of some midway position between living a full life and absolute asceticism, we feel our conscience clear whatever their choice' (p. 434). Freud then remarks that people who know the truth about themselves are permanently protected from the dangers of immorality even though their moral standards are different from the customary ones in society. Freud relates the widening of the intellectual horizons of the patient to 'the surprising and liberating enlightenment the treatment brings with it' (p. 440), which also increases the patient's capacity to make choices.

In the course of the last of the *Introductory Lectures* (Lecture 28) Freud sums up the nature of the therapeutic work which, he says, falls into two phases. The steps described for each of the phases can be considered to reflect aims of the psychoanalytic method as seen at that time.

> In the first [phase], all the libido is forced from the symptoms into the transference and concentrated there; in the second, the struggle is waged around this new object and the libido is liberated from it. The change which is decisive for a favourable outcome is the elimination of repression in this renewed conflict, so that the libido cannot withdraw once more from the ego by flight into the unconscious. This is made possible by the alteration of the ego[5] which is accomplished under the influence of the doctor's suggestion. By means of

---

5 Until 1923 Freud's concept of 'ego' was not the same as the 'ego' of his 1923 structural theory. In the earliest years the term stood either for the 'person', or for the 'self', or for consciousness (Rapaport, 1958). Later, in the first part of the phase dominated by the topographical theory, the notion of the ego as a set of forces (the 'self-preservative' ego instincts) was introduced, as well as the concepts of 'pleasure ego' and the opposing 'reality ego'.

the work of interpretation, which transforms what is unconscious into what is conscious, the ego is enlarged at the cost of this unconscious.

(1916–17, p. 455)

Freud also puts this point in a somewhat different way.

I will now complete my picture of the mechanism of cure by clothing it in the formula of the libido theory. A neurotic is incapable of enjoyment and of efficiency – the former because his libido is not directed on to any real object and the latter because he is obliged to employ a great deal of his available energy on keeping his libido under repression and on warding off its assaults. He would become healthy if the conflict between his ego and his libido came to an end and if his ego had his libido again at its disposal. The therapeutic task consists, therefore, in freeing the libido from its present attachments, which are withdrawn from the ego, and in making it once more serviceable to the ego. Where, then, is the neurotic's libido situated? It is easily found: it is attached to the symptoms, which yield it the only substitutive satisfaction possible at the time. We must therefore make ourselves masters of the symptoms and resolve them – which is precisely the same thing that the patient requires of us. In order to resolve the symptoms, we must go back as far as their origin, we must renew the conflict from which they arose, and, with the help of motive forces which were not at the patient's disposal in the past, we must guide it to a different outcome. This revision of the process of repression can be accomplished only in part in connection with the memory traces of the processes which led to repression. The decisive part of the work is achieved by creating in the patient's relation to the doctor – in the 'transference' – new editions of the old conflicts; in these the patient would like to behave in the same way as he did in the past, while we, by summoning up every available mental force [in the patient], compel him to come to a fresh decision. Thus the transference becomes the battlefield on which all the mutually struggling forces should meet one another.

(1916–17, pp. 453–454)

Thus the outcome of the 'struggle on the battlefield of the transference' leads ideally to the aim of the 'resolution of the transference'. This has, since Freud's earliest writings on analytic technique (see 1912, p. 118), been regarded as a major technical aim, in spite of the many changes which have occurred in psychoanalytic theory since that time.

After the *Introductory Lectures* Freud's views of the aims of psychoanalysis represent variations on past themes as well as new formulations. For example in 'Two encyclopedia articles' (1922a) he comments, 'The

17

removal of the symptoms of the illness is not specifically aimed at, but is achieved, as it were, as a byproduct if the analysis is properly carried through' (p. 251).

In 1923, in *The Ego and the Id*, Freud took a major theoretical step forward in his formulation of the 'structural' model of the mind in terms of the *id, ego* and *superego*. This new theory was intended to replace the earlier 'topographical' theory of 1900. The ego was now considered to be an organisation, an *agency* which mediates between the demands of the id, the superego and the external world. Freud saw the aim of analysis as being directed towards bringing about changes in the patient's ego ('ego' was used in the new 'structural' sense). For example, Freud remarks that 'analysis does not set out to make pathological reactions impossible, but to give the patient's ego *freedom* to decide one way or the other' (p. 50). And, in 'The question of lay analysis' (1926b), Freud says that as a result of the struggle against resistances, and overcoming them, the patient's ego is sufficiently altered and strengthened so that we need not be concerned about his behaviour after the end of treatment. With the introduction of the structural theory the focus of the analytic work was further extended from the aim of liberating repressed material in order to make it accessible and acceptable to the individual. So a major orientation of the analytic work was towards producing greater freedom of the ego from its 'three masters', i.e., the id, the superego and the external world.

Freud develops this view in the *New Introductory Lectures* (1933) when, in speaking of the therapeutic efforts of psychoanalysis, he says 'its intention is, indeed, to strengthen the ego, to make it more independent of the superego, to widen its field of perception and enlarge its organization, so that it can appropriate fresh portions of the id. Where id was, there ego shall be.[6] It is a work of culture – not unlike the draining of the Zuider Zee' (p. 80).

Nevertheless, in these lectures (1933) Freud once again shows his concern with the therapeutic goal of analysis. He points out the inevitable therapeutic limitations of psychoanalysis, and makes the statement (which was to become an extremely important issue in later years) 'that success can only be obtained when the treatment has been adapted to the characteristics of the illness' (p. 156). Here he expands the view, expressed years earlier in 'Lines of advance in psychoanalytic therapy' (1919), where he commented that there is a 'gradually growing appreciation that the various

---

6 Translations always provide problems. Loewald (1970) has pointed out that James Strachey's translation in the *Standard Edition* as 'where id was ego shall be' would be more appropriately rendered 'where id was ego shall become', giving Freud's statement more precision. In Loewald's view the phrase should be taken as implying that the id (or parts of it) change into ego, rather than that ego takes over territory previously belonging to the id.

forms of disease treated by us cannot all be dealt with by the same technique' (p. 165), and indicates that psychoanalytic technique still bore the hallmark of having developed in relation to the treatment of hysteria. This foreshadows ideas to be formulated later in 'Analysis terminable and interminable' (1937a).

In 'Constructions in analysis' (1937b) Freud makes his famous comparison between analysis and archaeology, and says 'for the archaeologist the reconstruction is the aim and end of his endeavours while for analysis the construction is only a preliminary labour' (p. 260). However, he adds that 'Quite often we do not succeed in bringing the patient to recollect what has been repressed. Instead of that, if the analysis is carried out correctly, we produce in him an assured conviction of the truth of the construction which achieves the same therapeutic result as a recaptured memory' (pp. 265–266).[7]

In this paper Freud takes up the further theme that analysis aims at the relinquishing of repressions belonging to the patient's early development and to put in their place psychically mature reactions. It is legitimate for the question to be asked here of whether 'maturity' is a notion equivalent to 'normality'. That Freud might have meant this is suggested by his assumption in 'Analysis terminable and interminable' (1937a) that what analysis achieves for neurotics is no more than what normal people have achieved for themselves without its help. However, this still leaves the problem of what normality implies. Does Freud imply that psychological maturity is an ideal developmental stage which patients with psychological disturbances have not reached? Any answer must inevitably be complicated by the fact that social value judgements are involved in the 'maturity' concept, and indeed Freud takes the view that it is impossible to define health except in metapsychological terms, i.e., by reference to the dynamic relations between the agencies of the mental apparatus. He also refers to the normal ego as being 'an ideal fiction'. Nevertheless, in discussing the idea of the 'end' of an analysis, Freud says that it is attained when no further change can take place. He says, 'It is as though it were possible by means of analysis to attain to a level of absolute psychical normality – a level . . . [which could] remain stable, as though, perhaps, we had succeeded in resolving every one of the patient's repressions and in filling in all the gaps in his memory' (pp. 219–220). Freud asks whether there is any possibility of this happening. In fact, he says, this can occur in some cases, and the neurotic

7 Freud's use of the term 'construction' in this paper is not entirely clear, as for the most part he uses the terms 'construction' and 'reconstruction' synonymously. The question of the role of reconstruction in the analytic process has assumed increasing importance in recent years (see Blum, 1994).

disturbance will have been cleared up, neither to return nor to be replaced. In such disturbances there has been no alteration of the ego, and the aetiology of the disturbance has been essentially traumatic. It is abundantly clear that Freud has a concept of 'normality' in mind when thinking of the aims of analysis, even though he has grave doubts about whether it could be achieved, except in a minority of cases. Even in 1904 Freud had remarked that 'it must be remembered that an ideal condition such as this is not present even in the normal, and further that it is only rarely possible to carry the treatment to a point approaching it. Just as health and sickness are not different from each other in essence but are only separated by a quantitative line of demarcation which can be determined in practice' (p. 253).

'Analysis terminable and interminable' is a remarkable paper on the conditions that affect the outcome of analytic therapy, and which explores the possibilities of change in relation to these conditions (see Sandler, 1991, for full discussions of Freud's paper). In this work Freud concentrated his attention on the *resistances* to change in and through analysis, and was clearly influenced in his formulation by Anna Freud's work on internal psychic conflict and the overriding need to analyse resistance and defence (Freud, 1936). He was anxious to set out his views on the aims and limitations of the psychoanalytic method, contrasting them with what he regarded as inadequate conceptions of analytic cure, as in the proposal of Otto Rank who, in his book *The Trauma of Birth* (1924), had put forward the idea that the patient's neurosis could be completely cured if only the primal trauma of birth were dealt with. Freud commented scathingly, saying that:

> We have not heard much about what the implementation of Rank's plan has done for cases of sickness. Probably not more than if the fire brigade, called to deal with a house that had been set on fire by an overturned oil lamp, contented themselves with removing the lamp from the room in which the blaze had started. No doubt a considerable shortening of the brigades's activities would be effected by this means.
>
> (1937a, pp. 216–217)

Freud asks whether, from a practical standpoint, an analysis is ended when the analyst and the patient cease to meet, and states that an appropriate ending occurs when two conditions have been more or less fulfilled. First (and this is worthy of note), the patient shall no longer be suffering from his symptoms and shall have overcome his anxieties and inhibitions; second, the analyst shall have judged that so much repressed material has been made conscious, so much that was unintelligible has been explained, and so much internal resistance conquered, that there is no need to fear a repetition of the pathological processes concerned. The question is then put by Freud of whether analysis accomplishes anything 'which does not, under favourable and normal conditions, occur of itself'. He answers, in the best Jewish tradition, with a new question: 'Is it not precisely the claim of our theory that analysis produces a state which never does arise spontaneously in the ego and that this newly created state constitutes the essential difference between a person who has been analysed and a person who has not?' (p. 227).

While in Freud's paper an aim of analysis is expressed as being the freeing of the patient from symptoms, inhibitions and character abnormalities (p. 216), the main emphasis remains on change in the ego. Freud sees the therapeutic alteration of the ego as the undoing of alterations already present as the result of the defensive process (see James Strachey's editorial note in Freud, 1937a, p. 211). This undoing allows instinctual drives that have not been successfully repressed to be permitted expression in the ego, subject to reliable ego-syntonic controls. For Freud, an aim of analysis is therefore something which may be described as a 'taming' of the instinct; that is to say, the instinct is brought completely into harmony with the ego, becomes accessible to all the influences of the other trends in the ego and no longer seeks to go its independent way to satisfaction.

Freud also considers the analytic task (and, because of that, its aim) from the point of view of the ego's defence mechanisms:

> The essential point is that the patient repeats these modes of reaction during the work of analysis as well, that he produces them before our eyes, as it were. In fact, it is only in this way that we get to know them. This does not mean that they make analysis impossible. On the contrary, they constitute half of our analytic task. The other half, the one which was first tackled by analysis in its early days, is the uncovering of what was hidden in the id. During the treatment our therapeutic work is constantly swinging backwards and forwards like a pendulum between a piece of id analysis and a piece of ego analysis. In the one case we want to make something from the id conscious, in the other we want to correct something in the ego.
>
> (p. 238)

Finally, Freud states:

> Our aim will not be to rub off every peculiarity of human character for the sake of a schematic 'normality', nor yet to demand that the person who has been 'thoroughly analysed' shall feel no passions and develop no internal conflicts. The business of the analysis is to secure the best possible psychological conditions for the functions of the ego; with that it has discharged its task.
>
> (p. 250)

21

To conclude . . .

Looking back on Freud's proposals in regard to aims one cannot fail to be struck by how preoccupied he was, explicitly or implicitly, with the topic, and how he moved as necessary from one conceptualisation to another. So while he was concerned with issues of cure, and of mental health and normality as aims of analysis, he was equally attentive to aims in the sphere of analytic technique, that is, aims relating to the analytic process itself. Freud never abandoned the therapeutic goal of analysis although he had difficulties with it, cautioning that the aim of curing the patient should not preoccupy the mind of the analyst, who should aim to apply the *method* of psychoanalysis. In so doing, internal psychic changes would be brought about and, as a side-effect, would also bring about a satisfactory therapeutic result. The subsidiary aims involved in the application of the psycho-analytic method show a progressive development from the simple formula of 'making the unconscious conscious', a development which took into account the increasing knowledge of ego functioning and the effects of analytic interventions on the way in which the different agencies of the mind act and interact.

We have referred to the tension throughout Freud's writings between the aim of curing and that of doing research and have considered Freud's (at times contradictory) attempts to resolve this conflict. But there was a further and equally dynamic tension between two opposing and more or less concurrent trends in his thinking. The first is an optimistic, at times even idealistic, view of what analysis can achieve; the other is a more realistic (one could say pessimistic) attitude, shown perhaps most clearly in 'Analysis terminable and interminable' (1937a). To some extent Freud's pessimism was linked with his view of the power of the death drive (1920), a concept formulated shortly after the end of the 1914–18 war, and which had profound repercussions on Freud's ideas about how much analysis can free the individual from his neurotic conflicts. The tension between optimism and pessimism runs right through the later psychoanalytic literature on aims.

Freud's death in 1939 coincided with the beginning of the Second World War. By then the literature included important contributions from a number of analysts, not all of whom were in total agreement with Freud. The next two chapters are concerned with some of these early contributions – milestones in the conceptualisation of aims and the psychoanalytic idea of mental health.

The early Freudians in the 1920s

The 1920s were very significant for psychoanalysis in a number of ways. Freud replaced his topographical theory with a new theory of the mind in 1923, and revised his theory of anxiety in *Inhibitions, Symptoms and Anxiety* in 1926. In this work the idea that anxiety was transformed libido was replaced by the concept of anxiety as a signal to the ego that some sort of danger threatened. These theoretical changes had profound implications for ideas about psychoanalytic technique, and for the relation between theory and practice. While before the 1920s Freud's psychoanalytic colleagues had for the most part echoed his various views on aims (even though some analysts, e.g. Jung, Adler, Stekel, had major disagreements with Freud about other theoretical ideas), in the 1920s the situation was rather different. Some significant Freudian analysts made substantial contributions to the ways in which Freud's new theoretical ideas could be applied to the conceptualisation of enduring psychic change as an aim of treatment. What was very striking was the consistent emphasis on the idea that this aim could only be achieved through modification of the superego, and that such modification comes about as a consequence of transference interpretation. A harsh superego, based on the introjection of strict parental attitudes, was regarded as a critical element in the formation of a neurosis. The parental aspects of the superego would be attributed to the analyst as part of the development of the transference, and appropriate interpretation would lead to a mitigation of the severity of the superego, and consequently greater health for the patient.

The position in the early 1920s has been well characterised by Fenichel (1941), who refers to the Scylla and Charybdis of analytic technique – too much talking versus too much feeling:

In the early days of psychoanalysis the [topographical] formula to the effect that in analysis 'the unconscious is made conscious' held sway. This formula was better known than the dynamic one, as yet not understood, that analysis must 'abolish resistances'. At that time, there-fore, the greater danger was the Scylla of too much talking or intellectualisation: the analyst guessed at complexes, named them and depended upon that for the cure. This might succeed if there were no special resistance isolating what was talked about from the actual point of the dynamic defence conflict. If there was such a resistance, the analyst relied in vain upon a comparison with the many cables that had to be untied one by one. As long as the main secret – resistance – remained unsolved, he might understand intellectually as much as he could about childhood and development but it did no good.

(1941, pp. 99–100)

In 1923 Sándor Ferenczi and Otto Rank published a book in German on *The Development of Psychoanalysis* (Ferenczi and Rank, 1925). In a chapter on 'A historical critical retrospect' they comment on how faulty it is to hold fast to the analysis of the patient's symptoms, and criticise the idea that cure can be brought about through the intellectual 'enlightenment' of the patient by explanation of his resistances. 'It was a comprehensible, but fatal mistake of some of our adherents to think that in the analysis the mere finding of the mistake in development should at once have a therapeutic effect; in contrast to this one-sided 'socratic' interpretation the actual effective remedy must be sought in properly connecting the affects with the intellectual sphere' (p. 51). Fenichel (1941), commenting on Ferenczi and Rank's book, which was, in his view, a reaction against 'the Scylla of too much talking or intellectualisation' says,

They emphasised again and again that analysis is not an intellectual but an affective process . . . in which emotional experiences are relived in the transference and previously hidden material thus revived for the ego's disposal. The authors certainly went too far to the other extreme. In their emphasis on experiencing they became admirers of abreaction, of acting out, and thus working through was the loser.

(1941, p. 100)

The issues raised by Ferenczi and Rank prompted a symposium two years later on 'The Relation of Psychoanalytic Theory to Psychoanalytic Technique', held in 1924 at the Eighth Congress of the International Psychoanalytical Association in Salzburg. This symposium produced important discussions of papers, including those presented by Hanns Sachs, Franz Alexander and Sándor Rado. It is noteworthy that this was the first Congress to take place after Freud's introduction of the 'structural' theory in *The Ego and the Id* (Freud, 1923), which was in fact adumbrated by Freud in a paper given at the International Congress in Berlin in 1922. In this paper (summarised in the *International Journal of Psycho-Analysis* in 1923) Freud is reported as having said that 'unconscious' was essentially a descriptive term, including also that which is known as 'preconscious', i.e., content that is latent but not repressed. There are disadvantages, according to Freud, to the double meaning of the term 'unconscious', i.e., the Unconscious of the topographical theory and 'unconscious' in its wider descriptive sense. The repressed should not be identified with the Unconscious, nor the ego with the Preconscious and Conscious systems. The reporter states: 'The speaker discussed the two facts which demonstrate that in the ego also there is an Unconscious, which behaves dynamically like the repressed Unconscious, these facts being, namely, the resistance which proceeds from the ego during analysis, and an unconscious sense of guilt' (Freud, 1922b, p. 367). Freud attempted to deal with these conceptual complications with his new 'structural' theory, involving the mental agencies (*Instanzen*) of id, ego and superego. This had profound implications for the topic of the symposium at the 1924 Salzburg Congress, and the views put forward there by Sachs, Alexander and Rado are worth considering in some detail.

Sachs, in his paper on 'Metapsychological points of view in technique and theory' (1925), refers to the influence of analytic technique on the patient's ego ideal (Sachs refers here to Freud's new concept of the superego).

> The end to be desired is, of course, that the patient should as far as possible adopt as his ego ideal the ideal put forward by analysis, first and foremost, perfect sincerity towards himself, removal of the repressions; that unperturbed by the idiosyncrasies and defects in the personality of the analyst, both in his [the analyst's] ego and in his superego, the patient should adopt the analyst's ideal of the analysis itself.
>
> (1925, p. 11)

The transference attaches itself to the personal characteristics of the analyst and this distorts the formation of the ego ideal. However, the analytic process, if it goes well, results in the following:

> The ego ideal which gradually emerges from the crucible of the transference comes to be gentler and more indulgent towards the ego and accustoms itself to recognise the ego's peculiarities and weaknesses and to take them into account instead of simply ignoring them, as hitherto, and issuing commands or prohibitions which were beyond its powers to obey. It is scarcely necessary to say that this process is of great therapeutic value.
>
> (1925, p. 12)

Franz Alexander, in 'A metapsychological description of the process of cure' (1925), points out that the change which we seek to bring about by analytic treatment is the recovery of health through changes in the ego.

> The object of the treatment is clearly to reverse the symptomatic gratification repudiated by the ego, to reestablish the original instinct-tension and to force the mental apparatus to make a fresh attempt at instinct-gratification, one in consonance with the requirements of the ego. The mind of the neurotic struggles against this by producing resistances to the treatment.
>
> (1925, p. 17)

The mental system may use either autoplastic or alloplastic mechanisms, and in neurosis we have 'a protest against the developmental tendency towards alloplastic modification' (p. 16). Here the term *alloplastic* refers to adaptive alterations by man of his environment, and *autoplastic* to adaptive internal changes made in order to accommodate to the demands of the external world (Freud, 1924).

However, in line with Sachs's views, Alexander's discussion of the aims of analysis and of the process of cure places much emphasis on the role of the superego in conflict and resistance:

> We now see that our therapeutic endeavours must be directed against this two-faced overlordship on the part of the superego. . . . The superego . . . is an anachronism in the mind. It has lagged behind the rapid development of civilised conditions, in the sense that its automatic, inflexible mode of function causes the mental system continually to come into conflict with the outer world. This is the teleological basis for the development of a new science, that of psychoanalysis, which, be it said, does not attempt to modify the environment but, instead, the mental system itself, in order to render it more capable of fresh adaptations to its own instincts. This task is carried out by limiting the sphere of activity of the automatically-functioning superego, and transferring its role to the conscious ego. This is no light task; it implies the conscious creation of a new function.
>
> (1925, pp. 23, 25)

The process of cure was seen by Alexander as being the overcoming of resistances to taking over the superego's *function* by the ego. He refers to Freud's view that 'the aim of treatment is to substitute judgment for repression', and comments:

> The task during treatment is to eliminate gradually the repressing institution, the superego: from the two component-systems, the ego and

the superego, a homogeneous system must be constructed – and this must have a two-fold perceptual apparatus, one at the outer surface directed towards reality, and one at the inner boundary directed towards the *id*. Only in this way can a mastery of instinct be achieved which is free from conflict and directed towards a single end.

(1925, p. 26)

Alexander points out that the analyst makes use of the transference, taking over the part of the superego, only in order to shift it back on to the patient again when the process of interpretation and working through has been carried out. The superego has arisen through a process of introjection of the relationship to those persons who in the first instance enforced adaptation. So it is made up to an important degree of parental commands and prohibitions. The relations between id and superego are thus a permanent crystallisation of the past relations between the child and its parents. Interestingly, he makes a reference to the 'id child', whose methods are always to provoke the parents, i.e., the superego, to unjust and overly severe punishment in order to do what is forbidden without any feeling of guilt. The analyst aims to take over the role of supervisor of the patient's instinctual life, in order to hand back the control gradually to the conscious ego of the patient. The nature of transference is that the intrapsychic relations between id and superego become relations between id and analyst. This is a new educative process in analysis.

> The demands of reality are, however, not communicated by means of orders and prohibitions, as previously happened under the sway of the superego, but by a 'super-personal' method, by logical insight, by accurate testing of reality. In this way the reliving of his past becomes abandoned by the patient himself, and the original instinctual demands, which in consequence of a personal judgement can no longer be experienced in the transference-situation, appear in the mind as memories.

(1925, p. 28)

The whole series of transference situations is seen as one in which the analyst plays ever-changing roles taken over from the superego. At the termination of the treatment, the patient's consciousness, which hitherto has been adapted only to testing reality, has to face new tasks.

Having learned during treatment the language of instinct, it must take over responsibility for the regulation of instinctual activities, a regulation which has previously been exercised by the superego operating automatically. During treatment the analyst has thought and interpreted instead of the patient: indeed, by reconstructing the past he has done some remembering in his stead. From now on all this must be the patient's own concern. In bidding goodbye to his superego he must finally take leave of his parents, whom by introjection he had captured and preserved in his superego.

(1925, p. 31)

The third contributor to the Salzburg symposium, Rado, in his paper on 'The economic principle in psychoanalytic technique' (1925), emphasises the importance of the dissolution of the transference neurosis. He is quite explicit in saying that 'restoration to health is the concern of our therapy' (p. 41). It is of some interest that Rado concerned himself in his paper with a theory of hypnosis, pointing out how it can effect a cure in the patient. Such cure through hypnosis can come about because the hypnotist is introjected as a 'parasite upon the superego', thereby affecting the superego's function. According to Fenichel (1941), Rado meant that analysis begins with the patient experiencing a state similar to hypnotic rapport, with the analyst being a temporary 'parasite' on the patient's superego (i.e., taking over the superego's role in relation to the ego of the patient) until the transference has ultimately been dissolved.

The great emphasis placed on the role of superego transformation as an aim of psychoanalytic therapy by Rado, Sachs, and even more strongly by Alexander, was a major shift in psychoanalytic thinking during the late 1920s and early 1930s. Their contributions in this context have not been as well recognised as those of James Strachey, whose paper 'The nature of the therapeutic action of psychoanalysis' (1934), essentially based on their contributions, introduced the concept of 'mutative interpretation', i.e., interpretation of the transference which effects superego change (see Chapter 3). Apart from the term, which has obtained popular appeal, Strachey's concept reflects the ideas which had been put forward in Salzburg a decade previously.

Not all the presentations to the symposium emphasised the importance of superego change as the aim of analysis. Thus Wilhelm Reich (1924a), at that time a leading figure in the psychoanalytic movement, echoed the view which had just been expressed in a paper 'On genitality' (1924b), that the aim of analysis should be the freeing of libido from fixation points and repression, resulting in the primacy of the genital zone. Somewhat later (1928), in discussing the degree to which changes in the patient's character can occur as a consequence of analysis, he said:

> The extent to which the actual result approximates the desired change depends, in each case, on a great number of factors. Qualitative changes of character cannot be achieved by the present-day means of psychoanalysis. . . . What can be achieved are quantitative changes which, if they go beyond a certain measure, equal qualitative changes. . . . In this manner, the whole being of the patient becomes 'different', a change

which is often more apparent to people who see the patient only occasionally . . . than to the analyst. The inhibited and self-conscious person becomes freer, the apprehensive more courageous, the over-conscientious less scrupulous, the unscrupulous more conscientious. Nevertheless, the person's 'personal note' never gets lost and continues to show through whatever changes have taken place.

(1928 [1950], pp. 117–118)

The Salzburg symposium, with the heavy emphasis placed on the achievement of changes in the superego and in its function, raises questions about the role of the analyst's value system in relation to the analytic process. For example, Sachs points out that in a successful analysis 'the patient should adopt the analyst's ideal of the analysis itself', i.e., the analyst's ideal of a 'normal' 'mentally healthy' patient. One may well ask to what extent this ideal is a reflection of the analyst's own values, values embedded in his own social, cultural and ethical background. To what extent do the analyst's introjected parental standards, reflecting, as they do in various ways, the culture of the time, and their views of 'right' and 'wrong', 'good' and 'bad', impinge on the 'analytic' values the analyst has in mind? We can add that insofar as such values are non-conflictual and integrated into the analyst's personality they are not normally questioned, yet must affect the aims of the analysis.

Emphasis on structural change was also placed after Salzburg by Sándor Ferenczi, a most important figure in the early days of psychoanalysis. He points out in 'The problem of the termination of the analysis' (1927) that his analytic experience has made him abandon the view that exposure of the phantasy lying behind a symptom is sufficient to bring about an analytic cure. A reconstruction, in the sense of a rigorous separation of reality and phantasy, is necessary. The patient gives up the phantasy sources of gratification in the analysis and looks round for other, more real sources of gratification. Ferenczi speaks of analysis as being a 'true re-education' in which the whole process of the patient's character formation must be followed back to its instinctual foundations. He says, somewhat lyrically,

Might not the patient, divested of his old character, dash off in characterless nudity before the new clothing was ready? Freud has demonstrated how unjustified is this fear, and how psychoanalysis is automatically followed by synthesis. In reality the dissolution of the crystalline structure of a character is only a transition to a new, more appropriate structure; it is, in other words, a recrystallization. It is impossible to foresee in detail what the new suit will look like; the one thing that it is perhaps possible to say is that it will be a better fit, i.e. that it will be better adapted to its purpose. . . . The far sharper severance between the world of phantasy and that of reality which is

29

the result of analysis gives them [the analysed persons] an almost unlimited inner freedom and simultaneously a much surer grip in acting and making decisions; in other words it gives them more economic and more effective control.

(1927 [1955], p. 81)

This is followed by the well-known statement that 'the proper ending of an analysis is when neither the physician nor the patient puts an end to it, but when it dies of exhaustion, so to speak' (p. 85).

Ferenczi makes an interesting differentiation of aims in regard to male and female analysands, one which would today be regarded as a typical example of culturally determined male chauvinist values.

Every male patient must attain a feeling of equality in relation to the physician as a sign that he has overcome his fear of castration; every female patient, if her neurosis is to be regarded as fully disposed of, must have got rid of her masculinity complex and must emotionally accept without a trace of resentment the implications of her female role.

(1927 [1955], p. 84)

In a further paper on 'The elasticity of psychoanalytic technique' (1928) Ferenczi suggests that the analyst can promise a prospective patient that 'if he submits to the analytic process, he will end by knowing much more about himself, and that, if he persists to the end, he will be able to adapt himself to the inevitable difficulties of life more successfully and with a better distribution of his energies' (1928 [1955], p. 90). In contrast to the emphasis placed on superego change, Ferenczi considers as insufficient the idea that the process of recovery 'consists to a great extent of the patient's putting the analyst (his new father) in the place of the real father who occupies such a predominant place in his superego, and his then going on living with the analytic superego thus formed' (p. 98). He then makes the remarkable statement:

I should like to add that it is the business of a real character analysis to do away, at any rate temporarily, with any kind of superego, including that of the analyst. The patient should end by ridding himself of any emotional statement that is independent of his own reason and his own libidinal tendencies. Only a complete dissolution of the superego can bring about a radical cure. Successes that consist in the substitution of one superego for another must be regarded as transference successes; they fail to attain the final aim of therapy, the dissolution of the transference.

(Ibid.)

30

Ferenczi has second thoughts, however. He indicates, at the end of his paper, that his technique does not aim at ridding the patient entirely of any kind of superego. Rather, his objective is 'to destroy only that part of the superego which had become unconscious and was therefore beyond the range of influence'. He has no objection to 'the retention of a number of positive and negative models in the preconscious of the ordinary individual. In any case he will no longer have to obey his preconscious superego so slavishly as he had previously to obey his unconscious parent imago' (p. 101).

To conclude . . .

The main emphasis in the 1920s was on the necessity for analysis to bring about a change in the patient's superego. However, Herman Nunberg, writing on 'Problems of therapy' (1928), brought together a number of formulations which had been put forward since Freud's creation of the structural theory, and summed up the situation as it was by the end of the 1920s. In regard to the aim of analysis he states that 'In the ideal case the changes brought about . . . involve the entire personality and are therefore as follows: *the energies of the id become more mobile, the superego more tolerant, the ego freer of anxiety and the synthetic function of the ego is restored.* Analysis is therefore *actually a synthesis*' (1928 [1948], p. 119). By the synthetic function Nunberg means the ego's capacity for construction and synthesis which 'impel man to the harmonious unification of all his strivings and to simplification and productivity in the broadest sense of the word' (1928 [1948], p. 136). This statement reflects a mood which was prevalent in the 1920s, and which can be discerned in the way in which the aims of analysis were formulated by Freudian analysts. These analysts for the most part possessed a high degree of social consciousness and were influenced by social movements striving for an ideal individual in an ideal society. Analysts such as Reich, Bernfeld, Aichhorn (and later Fenichel) were influenced by Marxist ideals and in their later writings tended to idealise both what psychoanalysis and Marxism could achieve.

The latter part of the decade brought about a consolidation of Freud's structural theory, in which the role of the ego as a structure mediating between the demands of the drives, the superego and the external world began to be spelled out. This development led, for example, to the formulations in Anna Freud's *The Ego and the Mechanisms of Defence* (1936) and in Heinz Hartmann's *Ego Psychology and the Problem of Adaptation* (1939b), two works (to be discussed in the next chapter) which laid the basis for the blossoming of ego psychology, mainly in the United States, after the Second World War.

3

Consolidation in the pre-war decade

In the 1920s and the early 1930s interest in psychoanalysis outside the boundaries of the main analytic groups centred in Vienna, Berlin and Budapest had increased, and a number of people were drawn to those cities in order to undergo a period of personal analysis. This resulted in the spreading of psychoanalytic ideas and practice to a number of countries in Europe and North and South America, although until 1939 the centre of development of psychoanalysis remained in Europe.

As we have seen, Freud had put forward his radical revision of psychoanalytic theory in the form of the structural theory of 1923, to which he added significant modifications in 1926. For many analysts who were accustomed to working with the topographical model, the full implications and ramifications of the structural theory took some years to absorb. An exception to this was the rapid acceptance of the concept of the superego (although it was for some time still referred to as the ego ideal), which had an immediate impact. The importance of the superego was shown in the Salzburg symposium as early as 1924. At the same time many analysts continued using prestructural concepts after the introduction of the structural theory, finding it difficult to abandon their topographical frame of reference. This resulted in a certain amount of theoretical confusion. So the notion of an ego ideal (as distinct from the superego) persisted, although Freud had specifically equated the two in *The Ego and the Id* in 1923. 'Ego ideal' now tended to be used to refer to the individual's ideal for himself (see Sandler *et al.*, 1963). In addition, the distinction between the Preconscious system (Pcs) of the topographical model (which is, descriptively speaking, unconscious) had previously been sharply distinguished from the system Unconscious (Ucs), but this distinction lost some of its force once the structural theory was introduced: the term 'the unconscious' tended to be used for everything that was, descriptively speaking, unconscious, and this led to many analysts equating everything that is unconscious with the system Unconscious. Alongside this the term 'preconscious' also persisted (as it does to this day) to refer to mental content that can readily be called into consciousness. More confusion also arose because the term 'ego', a structure or agency in the new theory which had certain functions, referred to what would now be called the 'self', i.e., one's own person related to as an object,[1] in the sense employed by Freud in his paper 'On narcissism: an introduction' (1914).[2] In spite of all these theoretical problems, psychoanalysis in the 1930s showed increased precision and differentiation in regard to the theory of mental functioning and its application to treatment.

We have seen that Rado, Sachs, and particularly Alexander (Chapter 2) had taken the view in the 1920s that the transformation of the patient's superego can be regarded as the main aim of an analytic treatment. As mentioned previously, Strachey's paper, 'The nature of the therapeutic action of psychoanalysis' (1934), taking up the same theme, introduced the concept of 'mutative interpretations'. These were transference interpretations relating to the 'here-and-now' of the analysis, and were thought to bring about a modification of the patient's superego; and Strachey, like others before him, saw the central aim of psychoanalysis as being the bringing about of such internal superego change. However, Strachey developed these ideas further in a contribution to the, by now famous, symposium on 'The Theory of the Therapeutic Results of Psychoanalysis', held during the Marienbad Congress in 1936.

Strachey's contribution to the symposium begins with the questions: What is the character of the therapeutic results of psychoanalysis and how are those results brought about? His response is that the distinctive feature of psychoanalysis compared with other methods is that the results of

---

1　Elizabeth Spillius comments that although Melanie Klein used 'ego' and 'self' interchangeably, it appears that she had a tendency to use 'ego' when she meant the 'self-who-acts', the 'I' of George Herbert Mead, in contrast to the 'me' (Spillius, personal communication).

2　In fact, Freud never distinguished between these two meanings of 'ego', and a formal distinction was only introduced later by the ego psychologists in the United States. In spite of this and other significant contributions, the ego psychologists maintained strict adherence to Freud's structural theory (Arlow and Brenner, 1964), but more recently this model of the mind has been seen to have important limitations (Sandler, 1974; Brenner, 1994).

Anna Freud was well aware that, unlike the American ego psychologists, she still found the topographical theory useful. She once commented that 'I must say that in my writing I never made the sharp distinction [between the topographical and the structural theories] that later writers made, but according to my own convenience I used the one or the other frame of reference. I definitely belong to the people who feel free to fall back on the topographical aspects whenever convenient and to speak purely structurally when that is convenient' (Sandler and Freud, 1985).

analysis have *depth* and *permanence*. Psychoanalysis results in *real* changes in the patient's mental functioning, and these changes, if the analysis is successful, bring about a progression to what Freud called the genital level, the final stage of libidinal development. (The attainment of so-called 'genital primacy' was for many years regarded by many analysts as a major goal of psychoanalytic treatment, and was equated not only with 'maturity' in the sexual sphere, but with maturity in *all* the main sphere's of the individual's functioning.) Clearly, definite value judgements are involved.

> A neurotic illness may be regarded as the product of an interference with the individual's normal process of growth. Then, if the interference is removed, the normal process of growth will be resumed. In other words, analysis enables the half-childish, half-dwarfed mind of the neurotic to grow towards adult stature. . . . It seems as though, when the individual reaches the complete genital level of libidinal development, the destructiveness of his id-impulses diminishes, his superego becomes correspondingly milder, and the relations between his superego and his ego reach a tolerable equilibrium. The neurotic's libidinal development is held up at some earlier stage, so that there is constant disharmony between the three parts of his mind. It may be possible to *mitigate* such a situation in various ways. But a *real* improvement will only occur if the hold-up in the patient's libidinal development can be removed. For, if this is done, he will continue to develop towards the genital level, at which his whole tendency to internal conflict will be automatically diminished.
>
> (1937, pp. 139–140)

In effect, the changes referred to by Strachey imply permanent modification of the superego. In his paper he goes on to discuss the 'vital importance' of transference interpretations which, through the effect of processes of introjection and projection as they occur in the transference, bring about such modification. In reiterating the position taken up by early Freudians a decade previously, Strachey makes it clear that for him the introjection of the analyst as a 'new' superego is central.

> It is true that the analyst, too, offers himself to the patient as an object and hopes to be introjected by him as a superego. But his one endeavour from the very beginning is to differentiate himself from the patient's archaic objects and to contrive, as far as he possibly can, that the patient shall introject him not as one more archaic imago added to the rest of the primitive superego, but as the nucleus of a separate and new superego. And he hopes that in the course of the analysis this new superego will gradually extend and infiltrate the original superego and replace its unadaptable rigidity by an attitude that is in closer contact

with adult conditions and with external reality. He hopes, in short, that he himself will be introjected by the patient as a superego – introjected however, not at a single gulp and as an archaic object, whether bad or good, but little by little and as a real person.

(1937, p. 144)

In addition to Strachey's paper, the Marienbad symposium was significant as an exposition of the essential elements of the analytic therapeutic process in that it brought together a variety of prevailing views. It is possible to extract further perspectives on aims from the other contributors, especially Edward Glover, Herman Nunberg, Otto Fenichel, Edmund Bergler and Edward Bibring. Their papers were published in the *International Journal of Psycho-Analysis* in 1937.

We can infer a specific analytic aim from Glover's contribution to the symposium, i.e., the freeing of instinctual derivatives that had been defended against and can subsequently be analysed and modified. The determining factors in the analytic process are listed by Glover as follows: gradual psychic reassurance, gradual new introjections, gradual widening of the range of displacements leading to slow and new adaptations and fractional projections given assent to by the ego.[3]

Nunberg's Marienbad paper elaborates his concept of the synthetic function of the ego (see Chapter 2). However, Fenichel, in his contribution, emphasises the analytic aim of modifying the ego's ill-adapted defences against instinctual forces, replacing them by better-adapted ones. He also points out that 'the old formula "We cure by making the unconscious conscious" is *topographically* conceived and there is a danger that in our technique we may do too scant justice to the *dynamic* and *economic* standpoints (1937, p. 138)'. Bergler suggests that analysis should aim at doing away with the process of magical omnipotent thinking in the patient. In Bergler's view one of the agents of therapeutic change in the analytic process is the modification of the patient's sense of guilt through the reintrojection of a modified, more benevolent superego.[4] Nevertheless, other changes are also seen as necessary:

---

3 The inclusion of 'fractional projections' as an implied desirable outcome of analysis is commented on in a footnote by Glover, who says: 'I have never been able to see why a wider distribution of projective processes should not have as beneficial an effect as the correction of archaic introjections. There is an unwarranted tendency to disapprove of projection as if it were a bugaboo rather than a mental mechanism' (1937, p. 131). It is certainly true that many people still think of introjective processes as "good", and projections as "bad".'

4 Even after 1923 many authors continued to use the term 'ego ideal' in the sense of 'superego'. Where appropriate the 'superego' has been substituted for 'ego ideal' in the discussion of their work, although not in direct quotations from their writings.

> What is achieved in analysis by way of rendering the superego more tolerant and lenient must be taken with a grain of salt, as the following argument proves. Before analysis the stern superego allowed the neurotic to fulfil his pre-Oedipal and Oedipal wishes under the disguise of symptoms, at the cost of suffering; after analysis the superego, though grown more tolerant, does not allow those who have been cured to take this way out. It does indeed become more lenient, but only on condition that they renounce their old wishes and turn their steps into normal paths.
>
> (1937, p. 156)

Bibring's presentation is of special interest. He points out that a theory of therapeutic results requires a supplementary theory of therapeutic *procedure*. Although the two are closely connected, it is nevertheless important to make a distinction between them.

> If this distinction is maintained, a theory of therapeutic procedure would have to deal with questions concerning the essential methods and principles of the procedure, whereas for a theory of therapeutic results the following questions would have to be considered: in what way do the *changes* arise which constitute cure, and on what are they based? There is a general and a special theory of cure, according to whether one investigates the general conditions which may on principle be assumed in all cases, or the special ones, which vary with different types of illnesses.
>
> (1937, p. 170)

Bibring's distinction between general and special theories of cure implies that a further distinction can be made between general and specific aims, the latter being aims related to the specific diagnostic category into which the patient falls. In regard to the *general* aims of therapy Bibring comments that it may be 'provisionally described as a change in the reciprocal relations between the various institutions of the mind. This alteration includes a change *within* these institutions, i.e. within the id, the superego, and, most especially and decisively, within the ego' (p. 171). He then discusses in remarkable detail the changes which need to be brought about within the patient in order to effect an analytic cure. In his account he stresses the need to strengthen the weak ego

> which is the main object of the therapeutical influence of analysis . . . the ego which was defeated in childhood by the dangers that threatened it; whereas the strength of the grown-up ego, which has remained untouched by disease, may be considered as a supporting factor of cure. This part is constantly being strengthened by the effects of analysis. The ego is obviously better able to meet situations

36

of danger . . . if it is uniform, i.e. without contradiction in itself. By giving its uniformity back to the ego we increase its ability to defend itself adequately against the dangers that threaten it from the three quarters [id, superego and external world] upon which it is dependent.

(1937, p. 189)

It is of interest that Bibring could not allow himself to extend the idea of modifying the theory of cure to take into account differences between patients within any one specific diagnostic category.

The Marienbad symposium clearly demonstrated the reorientation towards psychoanalytic technique brought about by Freud's structural theory, and the resulting reformulation of the aims of psychoanalysis in terms of internal structural change rather than simply 'making the unconscious conscious'. While Strachey emphasised the modification of the superego, other contributors stressed the aim of achieving alterations *within* the other psychic agencies as well, and in the relations of the ego to the id, the superego and the external world.

In fact, the importance of the relation between the individual and the external world had begun to be evident some years before in the work of Michael Balint. In a paper on 'Character analysis and new beginning' given at the Twelfth International Congress in Wiesbaden in 1932, Balint had put forward the point of view that a character trait can be regarded as a 'set, rigid form of reaction', which affected the patient's relations to others. He said,

In psychoanalytic treatment [the patient] will not only become acquainted with the origins of these [character] traits but also learn to regard them as defences. In this way he becomes able to abandon some of them which have now become useless and represent an obstacle, only historically justified, to harmless joy. That is the answer to the question of whether and how far analytic treatment is able to alter the character. . . . Our task is to free the person from his many compulsory rigid conditions of love and hate. . . . Our aim is therefore an elastic, practical adjustment to external reality, while – if possible – completely preserving the inner freedom.

(1932 [1952], pp. 170–171)

Balint now introduces the concept of the 'new beginning' which he sees as a change in the patient's behaviour (i.e., in his character). The aim of the analysis is then not simply to bring the patient to the point where he remembers the repressed, because even if the symptoms disappear he will not experience himself as cured.

What is still lacking is that he should finally drop the many conditions which he always had to impose in order to be able to love without anxiety. It is therefore not enough for the patient to know that in fact the object of these conditions was to protect him from the surrender, from the excitation which was too much for him; even if he also knows the trauma from which these conditions arose, he still has to learn anew to be able to love *innocently, unconditionally,* as only children can love. This dropping of condition I call the *new beginning.*

(1932 [1952], p. 165)

The concept of the 'new beginning' was further elaborated in a paper on 'The final goal of psychoanalytic treatment', presented to the Thirteenth Congress in Lucerne two years later in 1934. It discusses in particular the changes which occur in the patient in his relations to objects. The 'new beginning' is seen as a phase which comes into being just before the end of analysis, and its occurrence is an important criterion for the termination of the treatment.[5] Balint points out that in this phase long-repressed infantile wishes begin to emerge, and they can be openly admitted after the working through of resistances to them, and of the anxiety the infantile wishes bring about.

It is not until even later that their gratification is experienced as pleasure. I have called this phenomenon the 'New Beginning', and I believe I have established the fact that it occurs just before the end, in all sufficiently profound analyses, and that it even constitutes an essential mechanism of the process of cure. . . . If, however, both patient and analyst hold out, this passionate phase passes and in its place a true object relation, adjusted to reality, develops before our eyes. . . . And even later one must treat these newly begun relations indulgently so that they may find their way to reality and active love.

(1932 [1952], pp. 192–193, 198)

There can be little doubt that Balint was a pioneer in the specific emphasis he placed on improvement in relationships as a central aim of analysis, an emphasis which was to find its fullest expression among the object-relations theorists in Britain, and in other contemporary object-relations theories.

In a very different way the emphasis on the individual's interaction with the external world is reflected in two works which were to have a profound impact on the development of psychoanalysis – Anna Freud's *The Ego and the Mechanisms of Defence* (1936) and Heinz Hartmann's *Ego Psychology and the Problem of Adaptation* (1939b). Anna Freud's book drew attention to a whole spectrum of defensive measures employed by the ego

---

5 The concept of the 'analyst as a new object' is one which has remained important in psychoanalysis. See, for example, papers by Baker (1993) and Pfeffer (1993).

in its attempts to deal with inner conflict arising not only from the inner agencies of id and superego, but also as a consequence of the individual's interaction with the external world. The aim of analysis is seen in terms of establishing harmonious relations between id, ego, superego and the external world; it is essential for the achievement of such harmony that the ego and its mechanisms of defence be subjected to analysis.

> In analysis the defensive processes are reversed, a passage back into consciousness is forced for the instinctual impulses or affects which have been warded off and it is then left to the ego and the superego to come to terms with them on a better basis.
>
> (1936, p. 68)

Clearly, Anna Freud's view of the role of superego change through analysis differs from that expressed by Strachey. For Strachey the central analytic task emphasised bringing about changes *within* the superego by means of 'mutative' transference interpretations; for Anna Freud the central task was to analyse the ego's *defences* against conflict, including conflict involving the superego, in order to obtain more harmonious relations between the psychic agencies and between them and the external world.

> We have realised that large portions of the ego-institutions are themselves unconscious and require the help of analysis in order to become conscious. The result is that analysis of the ego has assumed a much greater importance in our eyes. Anything which comes into the analysis from the side of the ego is just as good material as an id-derivative. We have no right to regard it as simply an interruption to the analysis of the id. But of course anything which comes from the ego is also a resistance in every sense of the word: a force directed against the emerging of the unconscious and so against the work of the analyst.
>
> (1936, p. 26)

Hartmann's monograph has also had a profound influence, particularly on the development of the school of ego psychology in the United States. This work was first presented to the Vienna Psychoanalytic Society in 1937, and published in German in the *Internationale Zeitschrift für Psycho-analyse und Imago* in 1939. It was not translated into English until after the war. The first translation was an abridged version by David Rapaport, and published by him with commentary in 1951, in his *Organization and Pathology of Thought*. A later full and improved translation, also by Rapaport, appeared as a separate monograph in 1958. While a good number of the German-speaking psychoanalysts who had to emigrate from the Continent before the war were familiar with Hartmann's work, its influence was greatest in the United States after the war. However, it is presented here as it reflected an important pre-war development in psychoanalytic thought, and certainly had an influence abroad before it was translated, through the work of analytic theorists such as Anna Freud, Rapaport, Fenichel, Kris and many others.

Hartmann pointed out that increasing knowledge of the ego's functions has led to the conclusion that not all can be regarded as being derivatives of unconscious conflict, i.e., some are 'apparatuses' of primary autonomy. Further, some ego functions which may have been born of conflict acquire an independent status – these have a 'secondary' autonomy. The autonomous ego functions constitute the conflict-free sphere of the ego. In a profound departure from traditional psychoanalytic formulations he places great stress on the importance of ego functions in relation to successful and unsuccessful adaptation, including adaptation to the external social environment as well as to internal conflict. Hartmann's views are of such importance in regard to the aims of psychoanalytic therapy that they are worth considering *in extenso*.

> Adaptation may come about by changes which the individual effects in his environment . . . as well as by appropriate changes in his psychophysical system. Here Freud's concepts of alloplastic and autoplastic change are apposite. [See Chapter 2, p. 26, for comments on these terms.] Animals, too, change their environment actively and purposefully, for example, by building nests and dens. A broad range of alloplastic adaptations is, however, available only to man. Two processes may be involved here: human action adapts the environment to human functions, and then the human being adapts (secondarily) to the environment which he has helped to create. Learning to act alloplastically is certainly one of the outstanding tasks of human development; yet alloplastic action is actually not always adaptive, nor is autoplastic action always unadaptive. It is often a higher ego function which decides whether an alloplastic or an autoplastic action – and in either case, what specific alteration – is appropriate in a given situation. . . . A third form of adaptation, neither quite independent from nor quite identical with the alloplastic and autoplastic forms, is the choice of a new environment which is advantageous for the functioning of the organism.
>
> (1939b, pp. 26–27)

The view of adaptation put forward by Hartmann is complex, in that it includes both intrapsychic adaptation and adaptation to the social and interpersonal world; it should not be regarded as a simple passive acceptance of the demands of the social world. Moreover, beneficial adaptation to the social group may not coincide with beneficial individual adaptation, and vice versa.

In setting therapeutic goals the individual's interests will generally outrank society's, but this will no longer hold when we have broadened our point of view to include the needs of society. Conversely, an individual's natural characteristics which do not coincide with his own interests, etc., may be important for society.

(pp. 27–28)

The issue of adaptation requires a consideration of the possible criteria for the concept of mental health:

The solution is simple whenever freedom from symptoms and health can be equated. If we add the factor of enduring freedom from symptoms and resistance to disruptions, we are still in a realm which is easily dealt with empirically. . . . But beyond the range where these criteria can be applied, it is very hard to give a scientific definition of mental health, or to define the state to which we want to lead our patients by the means of psychoanalysis . . . health is, in part, a very individual matter. Finally, the commonly used criteria of health are obviously coloured by *Weltanschauung*, by 'health morality', by social and political goals.

(p. 80)

The question of health and normality had, in fact, been taken up by Ernest Jones some years earlier in a paper on 'The concept of a normal mind', first published in Schmalhausen's *The Neurotic Age* in 1931, and reprinted in the *International Journal of Psycho-Analysis* in 1942. Jones's paper is significant in that it is the first psychoanalytic paper to address itself primarily to considerations of 'normality', which are inseparable from consideration of the aims of the analytic work. Some of the ideas in that paper had in fact been foreshadowed years before in a short presentation by Jones entitled 'The attitude of the psychoanalytic physician towards current conflicts', read before the Fourth International Psychoanalytical Congress in Munich in 1913, and published in Jones's *Papers on Psychoanalysis*. The analyst has

the single aim of enabling the patient to arrive, on the one hand, at a more complete knowledge of himself, bringing with it more self-control and a greater capacity for adaptation; and, on the other, at the fullest possible measure of independence. If the physician goes beyond this aim and, assuming the position of a moralist, teacher, or guide, proffers a solution of the difficulty based on his own judgement and necessarily influenced by subjective factors, he thereby oversteps the limits of psychoanalysis, mistakes its mode of operation and stultifies its purpose.

(1918, p. 315)

In spite of Jones's warning about subjective factors, he was certainly aware of their constant influence on the analyst, affecting his concepts of mental health and of the 'normal mind'. In his 1931 paper on this topic Jones also points out that the relatively imprecise definitions of normality given by psychoanalysts fall into two main groups, i.e., those depending on the criterion of 'happiness', and those relating to adaptation to reality. He introduces the concept of 'efficiency', which stands midway between the two, and comments that it should be remembered that 'in using any concept of efficiency as a criterion of normality it is important to distinguish between merely external success in life, where opportunity plays such a large part, and internal success – i.e., the fullest use of the given individual's powers and talents' (p. 31).

Jones conceives of the individual's state of psychic balance, which is susceptible to disruption. Internal freedom in the sense of feelings can provide a sense of inner confidence and security, very different from the state which obtains in the neurotic. The psychological problem of normality ultimately resides in the capacity to tolerate suspending the fulfilment of wishes without renouncing them or reacting to them in defensive ways. 'We reach the conclusion that the nearest attainable criterion of normality is fearlessness' (p. 7). In 1936, in 'The criteria of success in treatment', he put his view forward again, saying (optimistically) that one may expect 'a confident serenity, a freedom from anxiety, a control over the full resources of the personality that can be obtained in no other way than by the most complete analysis possible' (1936 [1948], p. 382).

By the end of the decade we find a much clearer and more differentiated formulation of a psychoanalytic concept of mental health in a paper by Hartmann on 'Psychoanalysis and the concept of health' (1939a). In his view the concepts of 'health' and 'illness' always exert a latent influence on our analytic habits of thought. It is a mistake to think that these terms have no practical significance, because, depending on our concept of health, we recommend analysis and make decisions about termination. As differences in outlook in this sphere lead to differences in technique, it is necessary to clarify the terms 'health' and 'illness'. In earlier days it seemed simpler to define mental health and illness; the presence of the pathogenic conflicts leading to neurosis was a basis for the psychoanalytic differentiation between the two states. Later it was seen that such conflicts also existed in healthy people, and the 'choice between health and illness was determined rather by temporal and quantitative factors . . . the more we begin to understand the ego and its manoeuvres and achievements in dealing with the external world, the more do we tend to make [the] functions of adaptation, achievement, etc. the touchstone of the concept of health' (pp. 308–309). Health is not a purely statistical average, nor should the 'abnormal', in the sense that is a deviation from the average, be regarded as synonymous with 'pathological'.

Hartmann goes on:

> So long as we make freedom from symptoms . . . the criterion of
> mental health, it is comparatively easy in practice to arrive at a
> decision. Even by this standard there exists no absolutely objective
> basis for our judgement; for a simple answer is not readily forth-
> coming to the question whether a given psychical manifestation is in
> the nature of a symptom or whether on the contrary it is to be
> regarded as an 'achievement'. It is often a difficult matter to decide
> whether the pedantry or ambition of an individual or the nature of
> his object-choice are symptoms in a neurotic sense or character traits
> possessing a positive value for health. Nevertheless this standard does
> provide us, if not with a basis for objective judgement, at all events
> with a consensus of opinion which is usually sufficient for all practical
> purposes. But health as it is understood in psychoanalysis is something
> which means far more than this. In our view, freedom from symp-
> toms is not enough for health; and we cherish higher expectations of
> the therapeutic effects of psychoanalysis.

(1939a, p. 310)

Noting that 'a healthy person must have the capacity to suffer and to be
depressed', Hartmann adds,

> Our clinical experience has taught us the consequences of glossing
> over illness and suffering, of being unable to admit to oneself the
> possibility of illness and suffering. It is even probable that a limited
> amount of suffering and illness forms an integral part of the scheme
> of health, as it were, or rather that health is only reached by indirect
> ways. We know that successful adaptation can lead to maladaptation
> – the development of the superego is a case in point. . . . But
> conversely, maladaptation may become successful adaptation. Typical
> conflicts are a part and parcel of 'normal' development and disturb-
> ances in adaptation are included in its scope. We discover a similar
> state of affairs in relation to the therapeutic process of analysis. Here
> health clearly includes pathological reactions as a means towards its
> attainment.

(1939a, p. 311)

Hartmann's point of view that the well-analysed individual will be able to
tolerate suffering and depression, and other disturbances of inner equilibrium, is one which has frequently reappeared in the later literature on the
aims of treatment.

In applying general theoretical formulations regarding mental health,
such as Freud's 'where id was, ego shall be', Hartmann advises caution.
Such formulations cannot easily be made consistent with what analysts in

fact call 'healthy', particularly as 'theoretical standards of health are usually too narrow in so far as they underestimate the great diversity of types which in practice pass as healthy'. In a way that recalls Jones's warning about the influence of subjective factors in the analyst (Jones, 1931), Hartmann remarks:

> One gains an impression that individual conceptions of health differ widely among analysts themselves, varying with the aims which each has set for himself on the basis of his views concerning human development, and also of course with his philosophy, political sympathies, etc . . . descriptions of a healthy or 'biologically adjusted' individual, if we confine ourselves entirely to their broadest general outlines, reveal a pronounced development in two directions. In neither direction, it needs scarcely be said, is it merely a question of some subjective factor, some personal predilection achieving expression; they are the results of a rich harvest of clinical experience, and of much valuable experience of the analytical process of cure. These two directions emphasize as the goal of development and health on the one hand rational behaviour and on the other hand instinctual life.
>
> (pp. 312–313)

Hartmann is critical of the idea of 'the glorification of instinctual man' and, at the other end of the scale, the ideal of 'the perfectly rational man' as a psychoanalytic model of health. While there is some connection between reason and successful adaptation, we should not take it for granted that the recognition of reality is the equivalent of adaptation to reality – 'The rational must incorporate the irrational as an element in its design' (p. 314). Further, the psychoanalytic view of 'freedom of the ego', i.e., 'freedom from anxiety and affects, or freedom to perform a task', is 'no more than control exercised by means of the conscious and preconscious ego':

> The phenomenon which I am thinking of is even more clearly marked in those persons who, for fear of losing their ego, are unable to achieve orgasm. These pathological manifestations teach us that a healthy ego must evidently be in a position to allow some of its most essential functions, including its 'freedom', to be put out of action occasionally, so that it may abandon itself to 'compulsion'.
>
> (pp. 314–315)

The equation of conflict with mental illness is also criticised by Hartmann, who remarks that 'conflicts are a part and parcel of human development, for which they provide the necessary stimulus'. In addition, 'a measure which is successful in relation to defensive needs may be a failure from the standpoint of positive achievement, and *vice versa*. . . . The theory of the neuroses has always presented the mechanism of turning away from reality solely in terms of pathological processes: but an approach from the standpoint of the problems of adaptation teaches us that such mechanisms have a positive value for health' (pp. 315–316).

The conclusion reached by Hartmann is that the common psychoanalytic conceptions of mental health 'approach the problem too exclusively from the angle of the neuroses or rather they are formulated in terms of contrast with the neuroses'. He goes on to say,

> Mechanisms, developmental stages, modes of reaction, with which we have become familiar for the part they play in the development of the neuroses, are automatically relegated to the realm of the pathological – health is characterised as a condition in which these elements are absent. But the contrast thus established with the neuroses can have no meaning so long as we fail to appreciate how much of these mechanisms, developmental stages and modes of reaction is active in healthy individuals or in the development of those who later become so, i.e. so long as an analytical 'normal psychology' is still very largely non-existent. This is one of the reasons why it is precisely the analysis of conduct adapted to reality which is today considered of such importance.
>
> (1939a, p. 317)

The view of mental health expressed by Hartmann is consistent with his conception of adaptation, as described in his book (1939b). There he introduced the concept of adaptation to 'the average expectable environment', and this concept underlies his conclusion that 'We would insist that the processes of adaptation are always appropriate only to a limited range of environmental conditions; and that successful efforts at adaptation towards specific external situations may in indirect ways lead at the same time to inhibitions in adaptation affecting the organism' (1939a, p. 319). Health or illness are, in Hartmann's view, closely connected with the person's adaptation to reality and with his sense of self-preservation. Adaptation can only be seen 'in relation to something else, with reference to specific environmental settings. The actual state of equilibrium achieved in a given individual tells us nothing of his capacity for adaptation so long as we have not investigated his relations with the external world' (p. 318).

To conclude . . .

From 1933 the increasing persecution of psychoanalysis, a 'Jewish science', led to the emigration of most continental psychoanalysts during the late 1930s. This, and Freud's move to London in 1938 and his death in the following year, marked the end of an important phase in the history of psychoanalysis, and shifted the centres of analytic thinking and practice to Britain and the United States.

The 1930s saw a number of developments in that there was more precise elaboration of the changes in psychic structure thought to occur in and through psychoanalytic treatment. Whereas emphasis in the 1920s had been on superego change as an outcome of analysis, now the role of the ego was given greater prominence. In this regard the relation of the ego to the external world, particularly to the social world, was taken into account to an increased degree, and with this, questions of mental health and normality came more explicitly into the foreground. With the work of Anna Freud, and particularly that of Hartmann, the ground was laid for the post-war development of ego psychology. At the same time the roots of later object-relations theories could be discerned in the work of such analysts as Balint who, in his concept of the 'new beginning', came to see psychic change in terms of changes in the patient's object relationships. In general, the greater experience of actual analytic work led to a heightened awareness of, as Strachey called it in 1934, 'The nature of the therapeutic action of psychoanalysis', and consequently of the aims of that therapeutic action.

4

The emigration of analysts and a period of transition

The 1940s can be regarded as a period of transition, largely as a result of the disruption in the development of the psychoanalytic movement due to the war. It is appropriate to turn first to Otto Fenichel whose work provides a useful bridge to the pre-war period. Fenichel had contributed a number of early papers on psychoanalytic technique (e.g. 1934, 1935), and had presented at the Marienbad symposium (1937), but his two major works, *Problems of Psychoanalytic Technique* (1941) and *The Psychoanalytic Theory of Neurosis* (1945), were written in wartime, when Fenichel, like so many other refugees, had emigrated to the United States. Fenichel was especially adept at pulling together the developments in psychoanalytic theory and technique of the pre-war decade. In his writings he maintained the emphasis placed by Freud (e.g. 1937a, 1940) and others in the 1930s on the need to bring about changes in the ego as an aim of analytic treatment.

> The therapeutic task then is to reunite with the conscious ego the contents (both portions of instinct and unconscious anxieties of the ego) which have been withheld from consciousness and the total personality by countercathexes of the ego, and to abolish the effectiveness of the countercathexes. . . . If the energy which was bound up in the defence struggle is joined again to the personality, it fits itself in with it and with the genital primacy arrived at by it. The pregenital sexuality, freed from entanglement in the defence struggle, is thereby changed into genital sexuality capable of orgasm.
>
> (1941, pp. 17–18, 21)

Fenichel goes on to say of psychoanalysis that

> Gradually it confronts the ego with contents previously warded off and abolishes the division between these isolated contents and the personality as a whole. It allows the instincts warded off to catch up with the development which the ego has passed through in the

47

meantime, changing infantile into adult sexuality, and thus makes possible a well regulated sexual economy. It leads to 'condemnations' of certain instinctual satisfactions by the reasonable ego and, finally, to sublimations. Everything else is incidental.

(1941, p. 23)

Later, in 1945, he remarks that psychoanalysis is 'not a single operation resulting in a single act of abreaction; it is, rather, a chronic process of working through, which shows the patient again and again the same conflicts and his usual way of reacting to them, but from new angles and in new connections' (p. 31). In addition,

> In sharp contrast to all other types of psychotherapy, psychoanalysis attempts the real undoing of the pathogenic defences. This is the only means of freeing the patient of the bad consequences of his pathogenic conflicts for good, and of placing again at his disposal the energies that hitherto have been bound in this conflict. Thus psychoanalysis is the only *causal* therapy of neuroses. Its aim is achieved by making the patient's ego face what it had previously warded off. The transference is not immediately used for therapeutic aims but is rather analysed; that is, its true nature is demonstrated to the patient.
>
> (1945, p. 569)

Fenichel's discussion of the aims of analysis was in the tradition of theory constructed on the basis of the experience of individual analysts in their consulting rooms. A somewhat different approach was evident in a paper read by Robert Knight in 1941 to the American Psychiatric Association (Knight, 1942) in which he considered the difficulties in formulating the criteria for evaluating the outcome of psychoanalytic treatment. His comments on these criteria and the corresponding aims of psychoanalysis are worth quoting in some detail as they reflect the fact that the profession of psychoanalysis had become in a sense a part of general psychiatry. American psychiatry was certainly influenced by the pragmatism of such pioneers as Adolf Meyer, whose psychobiological and mental-hygiene approach emphasised the relation of the individual to the community. Clearly, in Knight's paper we can perceive the effect of the needs and pressures of the American medical establishment at the time in the form of a composite schema of behavioural and intrapsychic criteria of change – indeed, the very way in which he constructed a formal list of criteria could be taken to be a sign of a particular scientific attitude.

According to Knight, any general statement of the aims of psychoanalytic therapy would include (p. 436):

1 Disappearance of the presenting symptoms.
2 Real improvement in mental functioning:

(a) the acquisition of insight, intellectual and emotional, into the child-hood sources of conflict, the part played by precipitating and other reality factors, and the methods of defence against anxiety which have produced the type of personality and the specific character of the morbid process;

(b) development of tolerance, without anxiety, of the instinctual drives;

(c) development of ability to accept one's self objectively, with a good appraisal of elements of strength and weakness;

(d) attainment of relative freedom from enervating tensions and talent-crippling inhibitions;

(e) release of the aggressive energies needed for self-preservation, achievement, competition and protection of one's rights.

3 Improved reality adjustment:

(a) more consistent and loyal interpersonal relationships with well-chosen objects;

(b) free functioning of abilities in productive work;

(c) improved sublimation in recreation and avocations;

(d) full heterosexual functioning with potency and pleasure.

In spite of the picture of what psychoanalysis can achieve painted by the aims listed in his paper, Knight showed his awareness of the limitations of analysis, He introduces a realistic note when he says:

> It is an entirely illogical and unfair expectation for the patient, his friends, relatives or referring physician to anticipate that after being treated by the method of psychoanalysis he will become a paragon of all the virtues and accomplished without flaw, defect or anxiety and capable of behaving in every possible situation like a superman. Yet psychoanalytic therapy is often judged by these very criteria. One might as well expect that psychoanalysis would also cure his freckles, his bad golf swing and his aversion to turnips. No, the patient will remain essentially the same person after the best analysis – rid of his disabling symptoms, perhaps, or able to handle what ones are still left, more adaptable, more productive, happier in his relationships, but still the same person as to native endowment, appearance and basic temperament.
>
> (1942, p. 437)

He suggests five 'reasonable criteria' for measuring the success of an analysis, in addition to taking into account the patient's own limitations, the severity of his illness and the duration of the analysis. These criteria are:

1 symptomatic recovery, i.e., relative freedom from or significant diminution of disabling fears, distress, inhibitions, dysfunctions, etc.;

2 increased productiveness, with improved disposition of his aggressive energies in his work;

3 improved adjustment to and pleasure in his sexual life;
4 improved, less ambivalent, more consistent and loyal interpersonal relationships;
5 achievement of sufficient insight to handle ordinary psychological conflicts and reasonable reality stresses.

Knight's delineation of 'realistic criteria' can be regarded as a way of conceiving the aims of psychoanalytic therapy which is very different from the *intrapsychic* changes emphasised in previous years as desirable outcomes of analysis. Although it could be argued that Knight's 'reasonable criteria' are superficial, in that they are tied to observable behaviour, they do represent an attempt to provide a basis for a relatively objective assessment of the outcome of psychoanalytic treatment, but do not contribute to a theory, in terms of psychoanalytic psychology ('metapsychology'), of desired *internal* change. Here we can perceive the influence of objectivism in American psychiatry, and the cultural emphasis at the time on fitting in well with the outer-directed tendencies in American culture, which is in marked contrast to, for example, the more inner-directed orientation of Europeans (see Riesman *et al.*, 1950).

Immediately after the war psychoanalysis in the United States developed rapidly within the framework of the ego psychological version of Freud's structural theory, and the next important step in the evaluation of therapeutic results took place in 1948 in a symposium at the Boston Psychoanalytic Society (Oberndorf *et al.*, 1948).

In this symposium Clarence Oberndorf referred to a questionnaire that he had distributed to experienced psychoanalytic physicians some years earlier, and on which he had reported at a meeting of the American Psychoanalytic Association in 1943 (Oberndorf, 1948).[1] Of direct relevance to the aims of psychoanalysis is Oberndorf's question of whether a successful outcome is represented by the alleviation of a symptom or a reconstruction of the personality. He gives the example of impotence cured to the level that a man could have intercourse with a prostitute but with no one else. According to some criteria this might be regarded as an analytic cure. Oberndorf cites a further case of a homosexual patient which one analyst might regard as having a successful outcome were the patient to be content with his homosexuality, but another analyst might feel that a satisfactory outcome would be conditional on the patient making a heterosexual attachment. In passing, it is worth noting that the achievement of

---

[1] Before the war an attempt had been made to evaluate the results of psychoanalytic therapy in a systematic way at the Berlin Institute. Although this study involved an assessment of the various degrees of improvement of patients in analysis, it was not particularly linked with formulations regarding the aims of analytic treatment.

heterosexuality by homosexuals was, until relatively recently, regarded as an aim of analysis by many analysts, and – surprisingly – is still so regarded by some. So what is seen as a successful outcome by one analyst may be unsatisfactory for another. Consequently the issue was raised of whether analytic cure is to be judged by the patient or by the physician.

Oberndorf's comments pinpoint a problem, which had been noted in the 1930s, that there is a distinction between the notion of an ideal state of mental health and 'attainable' mental health. The analyst's *Weltanschauung* and his capacity for being realistic about what analysis can achieve began to emerge more clearly as major influencing factors in considering aims.

Lawrence Kubie's remarks in this symposium extend this point by reference to *factors within the patient*. He comments that

> each individual patient who is under treatment represents not merely a process of illness but also a complicated constellation of social forces. He is a human being, with a certain kind of neurosis and personality. Also at the same time he lives in a certain type of milieu, subjected to a large number of variable external forces (i.e. social, educational, cultural, economic and family). Also he comes to treatment not alone, but trailing along behind him all of the feelings and attitudes, fears and pressures, resentments and hostilities, hopes and prayers, of those who constitute the human setting of his life. And on top of all of that he brings his own intricate processes of illness, with its medley of inter-related symptoms. Each of these variable elements makes up the agglomeration that we call a patient, and each variable has an influence on the effectiveness of any therapeutic technique.
>
> (Oberndorf *et al.*, 1948, pp. 16–17)

Phyllis Greenacre, too, emphasises the multiplicity of the factors influencing what psychoanalysis can achieve, stressing the constitutional elements. She sees these as 'the genetic neurotic elements which must be present in every individual, due to the discrepancies between the slow processes of inner biological change and the sometimes more rapid changes in environmental demands'. Greenacre adds, 'I am inclined to believe that in disregarding these, the psychoanalyst not only reverts to the naive lay attitude, but that this too is part of a narcissistic need to seek or to have omnipotence' (Greenacre, 1954, p. 13).

In spite of such personal needs on the part of analysts, it was probably inevitable that the pressure to assess the outcome of analysis in an 'objective' way, in order to show its value in comparison with other treatments, would lead to a certain de-idealisation and to a more realistic appraisal of what analysis could achieve. What we see in this pragmatic tendency is a strengthening of Freud's own at times cautious approach to the aims of psychoanalysis (which contrasted markedly with the highly idealised and optimistic view of what analysis can achieve that he expressed at other times).

In Britain the situation was rather different from that obtaining in the United States. In 1938, Freud had emigrated to London with his family from Austria, and soon Anna Freud, together with a number of predominantly continental colleagues, represented an analytic group within the British Society. Inevitably tensions arose between them and the group of British colleagues who were associated with or had been heavily influenced by Melanie Klein, who had come to England in 1926. Not all the analysts in the Society belonged to either of the two groups, others being in the so-called Middle Group. The differences between the groups led by Melanie Klein and Anna Freud were substantial in regard to the theory of child development and the approach to the use of interpretation in analysis. Klein saw pathology as being developmentally rooted in the first months of life. She placed emphasis on the persistence in later life of very early unconscious phantasies, on the move from what she later came to designate as the 'paranoid-schizoid position' (1946) to the 'depressive position', and the consequent working through of the latter position. Klein's emphasis on the positive therapeutic value of mourning processes and on the 'repair' of the damaged internal object is probably reflected in her psychoanalytic technique. Anna Freud adhered much more to the 'classical' psychoanalytic view of development, placed within the framework of Freud's structural theory, with special emphasis on the role of the ego and the analysis of the mechanisms of defence. In this, as in all her work, her early training as a teacher was discernible.

The radical differences between the approaches of Anna Freud and Melanie Klein, particularly in relation to the theory of infant development and the nature of unconscious phantasy, had profound implications for analytic technique, and consequently raised problems in regard to the training of analytic candidates. Compromises in regard to training procedures and curriculum were reached following the 'Controversial Discussions' which took place in the early 1940s. (A comprehensive overview of the situation at the time and of the discussions which followed has been given by King and Steiner, 1991.) Since then a *modus vivendi* has been established as a consequence of the 'gentlemen's agreement' reached between the three groups, now known as the Contemporary Freudians, the Independents and the Klein group.

Many of the members of the British Society were not physicians, nor even psychologists, but came from a variety of professional as well as cultural backgrounds, so the tie to the medical establishment and the need to evaluate the outcome of psychoanalytic treatment was not pressing. Until recently the British Society has had a noticeable bias against psychoanalytic research other than that carried out with the patient in the analyst's consulting room. In spite of this, some of the problems regarding the outcome of analytic treatment preoccupying analysts in America were in the minds of their colleagues in Britain as well. However, in Britain questions about outcome were not reflected in a wish to undertake formal research, but were evident in concerns about analytic procedures. This is well exemplified in a series of short papers on problems of termination of analysis, presented to the British Psychoanalytical Society in 1949. The participants were Michael Balint, Harold Bridger, Willi Hoffer, Melanie Klein, Sylvia Payne, John Rickman and Marion Milner, all of whose contributions were published in 1950. Presentations about termination are particularly useful in regard to the clarification of analytic aims, for they are closely tied to the actual clinical experience of analysts, and for the most part are not severely distorted by idealised notions of what analysis can achieve.

All the contributors to the series provide a statement of the aims of analysis from their different viewpoints. Melanie Klein (1950) indicates that the criterion for termination of an analysis (and therefore the implicit analytic aim) is to reduce persecutory and depressive anxieties sufficiently (i.e., to diminish the influence of persecuting internal objects), and to strengthen the relation of the patient to the external world well enough to allow him to deal satisfactorily with the situation of mourning arising at that point. This new perspective links with criteria of heterosexual potency, as well as the capacity for love, object relations and work. But, Klein stresses, improvement in these capacities is dependent on the lessening of persecutory and depressive anxieties.

Hoffer, an associate of Anna Freud, takes the view that analysis aims at increasing the degree of awareness of unconscious mental processes (Hoffer, 1950) Resistances have to be noticed and interpreted, repression and resistance against the repressed must be reduced, and there should be an increase in preconscious and perceptual mental activity. There has to be a change from acting out, as it emerges in the transference situation, into remembering. The aim of analysis is then to limit the scope of the transference neurosis by widening the knowledge of the patient's past and reducing the need to repeat it in the present. He also refers to what has been called the substitution of the patient's infantile superego by the analyst's superego, but sees it as a change in the patient's ego through identification, resulting in a modification of the patient's ideals for himself rather than directly affecting the superego.[2] However, he emphasises that

---

2 Hoffer correctly distinguishes the ego ideal (which we would now call the ideal self) from the superego, although some analysts equate the two (see Sandler *et al.*, 1963).

the mechanism involved is identification with the *functions* of the analyst. The patient identifies with the analyst's skill in interpretation, in analysing resistances and in transforming acting out into memories. Finally, he says that 'Individual analysis is the study of individual histories. History can never be exhausted, but its study does not always need two people. Treatment can be terminated when the analytic process can hopefully be entrusted to the apprentice himself' (1950, p. 195).

The views of Balint, who had emigrated to London from Budapest, and who was one of the outstanding figures of the Middle Group, are of special interest because they are connected with the paper he had presented in Wiesbaden in 1932 (Balint, 1932 [1950]), where he elaborated his concept of the 'new beginning'. They also show the growing emphasis in the British Society on object-relations theory. For Balint, psychoanalytic aims involve a firmly established genital primacy and the capacity to enjoy genital satisfaction. This capacity is seen as a function normally emerging at about the time of puberty, and in analysis the attainment of this capacity relates to the changing of an indifferent or even reluctant object (the patient) into a loving and cooperating genital partner. The patient allows increased rights to his objects by developing his ability to test reality in relation to his objects, and in this way tries to find an acceptable compromise between his own and their demands. The new beginning is a sort of rebirth into a new life, the patient arriving at the end of a dark tunnel, seeing the light again after a long journey.

Balint then raises an important question. He asks whether the state of health is the result of natural processes which would take charge of the cure if only the obstacles in its way created by the person and by social traumas could be removed:

> We have excellent theoretical criteria to decide whether an analysis has been properly terminated or not. Unfortunately we must admit that they are rather perfectionist standards, and we are not able to define what would constitute an admissible deviation from our criteria. . . . On the practical side, when examining the end phases of my truly terminated analyses, we landed in the dilemma: is health a 'natural' state, or is it only the result of extremely good luck, a very rare event? And we had to admit our inability to solve it.
>
> (1932 [1950], pp. 198–199)

To conclude . . .

Clearly, in the transition period of the 1940s, the interest in aims was to some extent prompted by concern with the outcome of psychoanalytic treatment. However, we can also see, particularly from the papers on termination, that the pressure to formulate aims also derives from conflict between different theoretical positions and technical procedures, and the consequent need to provide an appropriate rationale for them.

5

The 1950s and the widening-scope discussions

The 1950s saw a burgeoning of psychoanalytic theory and practice in a great many countries. After the disruption caused by the war, the immediate post-war years provided an opportunity for the training of many psychoanalysts and for the establishment and growth of psychoanalytic societies and institutes. Psychiatry, to varying degrees in different countries, was being influenced by psychoanalysis, and – as we saw in the previous chapter – this was particularly the case in the United States and Britain, where a number of psychiatrists who had served in the armed forces completed psychoanalytic training after the end of the war (see Gitelson, 1951, for a discussion of the relation between psychoanalysis and 'dynamic psychiatry' in the USA). The growth of the psychoanalytic movement also stimulated the development of analytically orientated psychotherapy, and it was inevitable that interest began to be focused more precisely on the differences between such therapies and psychoanalysis. As we shall see, the application of psychoanalysis beyond the neuroses led to a further awareness of the limitations of the analytic method and to increasingly open consideration of these limitations, accompanied by a degree of de-idealisation by psychoanalysts in relation to what analysis could achieve. It is worth noting that in 1950 Edith Buxbaum drew attention to the 'interminability' of the analyses of patients with character neuroses, and pointed out that, with such patients, we need to settle for certain limited results. She distinguished between a *therapeutically* satisfactory and an *analytically* satisfactory termination of analysis, reinforcing a distinction made earlier by others, and more recently by Oberndorf (Oberndorf, 1950), referred to in the previous chapter. Indeed, such a distinction, which represented a growing climate of pragmatism, played an increasingly important role in later discussions of analytic aims.

We have seen how during the 1940s analysts in the USA had become interested in the aims of psychoanalytic therapy because of the pressure of the medical establishment's interest in the outcome of treatment. In the succeeding decade the concern with therapeutic aims continued and became linked to issues of psychoanalytic technique. A major influence in analytic thinking at this time was the development of psychoanalytic ego psychology, which had come to dominate American psychoanalysis under the leadership of Heinz Hartmann, Ernst Kris and Rudolph Loewenstein. Ego psychology, according to *Psychoanalytic Terms and Concepts*, published by the American Psychoanalytic Association,

> covers all areas of study, research, theory building, and clinical application that place major emphasis on, and are presented from, the vantage point of the ego. Early psychoanalysis focused mainly on drive or id psychology, the unconscious, and conflict, with more or less *pari passu* references to the ego as personality, self or defence (repression). In the early 1920s Freud's structural theory and delineation of resistances established ego psychology as a major focus of the new science of psychoanalysis. Anna Freud's study of ego defences and Hartmann's elaboration followed. These developments opened the theory to research into psychosocial and constitutional considerations, thus enhancing the claim that psychoanalysis is a general psychology of the mind.
>
> (Moore and Fine, 1990, pp. 65–66)

'Ego' in this context refers to a psychic structure, an agency, to be distinguished from the mental representation of the self. The ego has the role of mediating between the drives and the superego on the one hand, and the external world, on the other. Its major function can thus be seen to be one of intrapsychic adaptation, and in this connection the workings of the ego itself came under scrutiny. Ernst Kris (1956) described the effect of the ego-psychological emphasis on the ego as follows:

> A random survey would, I believe, support the impression that in most recent writings on technique problems concerning the functions of the ego have been of increasing importance. However, within this broad area a shift of emphasis seems to be noticeable: while we were at first largely concerned with the intersystemic functions of the ego, i.e. the ego in its relation to id and superego, more recently interest in its intrasystemic functions has been added. Thus the interest in defence, as manifested in resistance, has been supplemented by some considerations concerning the integrative (synthetic) ego-tendencies, which are more regularly concerned with both inter- and intra-systemic conflicts.
>
> (1956, p. 446)

The perspective of ego psychology in the USA quickly became the 'establishment' point of view, and this was reflected in the teaching provided in most Institutes of the American Psychoanalytic Association. The focus on the ego, with the new attention to its functions and its capacity to develop its own autonomy, affected the theory and practice of psychoanalysis and the formulation of analytic aims in the United States, and to a lesser extent elsewhere. Kurt Eissler's well-known paper on 'The effect of the structure of the ego on psychoanalytic technique' (1953) was particularly influential in this context, in that it spelled out a 'standard' technique which had the analyst's interpretation as its main therapeutic tool. Deviations from what he called 'the basic model of psychoanalytic technique' were referred to as 'parameters' of technique, and such deviations (e.g. the patient sitting up rather than lying down) were regarded as temporary expedients which had to be interpreted. While this approach contributed to a rigidifying of psychoanalytic technique, the idea of 'parameters' in practice probably legitimised certain departures from strict analytic procedure, which were not necessarily 'analysed away' in the course of the treatment, but which were found to be therapeutically useful. In Eissler's view, psychoanalytic techniques (and consequently the implicit conceptualisation of aims) 'depend chiefly on three variables: the patient's disorder and personality, the patient's present life circumstances, and the psychoanalyst's personality' (p. 105). In this connection he adds that 'No individual can divorce himself from the historical period in which he is living any more than he can put himself beyond time or space' (p. 107).

Throughout Eissler's paper there is an emphasis on the need to take the state of the analytic patient's ego into account, and he points to the problem resulting from the fact that 'a patient often prefers to produce adjusted behaviour instead of a structural change' (p. 126). The patient may be 'obedient', says Eissler, and may produce improvements under the pressure of the therapy 'which are not based on the dissolution of the corresponding conflicts' (p. 126).[1] In spite of Eissler's strict ego-psychological approach, he is aware that analysis cannot change the structure of the ego fully, and that any attempt to do so can be characterised as 'heroic'.

The dominance of the ego-psychological perspective in psychoanalysis can be seen again in a presentation by Leo Rangell (1954) of the work of a Committee on the Evaluation of Psychoanalytic Therapy which had been established by the American Psychoanalytic Association in 1947. In reporting on the subsequent work of this committee Rangell characterises psychoanalysis as

---

[1] We can include here what Barchilon pointed out in regard to so-called 'countertransference cures' (1956), that in some severely disturbed patients who have dramatic recoveries the cures may be illusory and a consequence of unconscious wishes on the part of the therapist.

58

a method of therapy *whereby* conditions are brought about favourable for the development of a transference neurosis, in which the past is restored in the present, *in order that*, through a systematic interpretative attack on the resistances which oppose it, there occurs a resolution of that neurosis (transference *and* infantile) *to the end* of bringing about structural changes in the mental apparatus of the patient to make the latter capable of optimum adaptation to life. . . . Psychoanalysis aims at the establishment of the reaction (transference neurosis) and the maintenance of optimum conditions for its final complete resolution. It is not only oriented towards such a final end point, but, in contrast to psychotherapy is potentially capable of obtaining it. Psychotherapy, on the other hand, either from necessity or from choice, introduces the external agent and brings the reaction to an end at any intermediate point of stability.

(1954, pp. 739–40, 743)

Rangell closes with the statement that 'there is a spectrum of patients who require one or the other method and a spectrum of therapists able to do one or both. And there is a borderland of conditions, with great fluidity, which may at times call for a change of the technical approach in either direction' (p. 744).

Although Rangell presents a somewhat idealised ego-psychological point of view of the differences between the goals of psychoanalysis and those of psychotherapy, his final comments are in line with the views expressed in a symposium on 'The widening scope of indications for psychoanalysis' (1954) in which papers presented by Leo Stone and Edith Jacobson were discussed by Anna Freud. Stone describes the widening scope as 'a movement toward the broadening and multiplication of the psychoanalytic spheres of interest in the personality, and an appropriate complication of psychoanalytic technique' (Stone, 1954, pp. 567–568), referring here to child analysis and to the treatment of delinquency, perversion (Stone includes homosexuality), paranoia, schizophrenia and psychosomatic disorders, as well as 'that vast, important and heterogeneous group – the 'borderline" cases' (p. 568). He comments that 'there is an almost magical expectation of help from the [psychoanalytic] method, which does it grave injustice' (p. 568). Stone presents a 'classical' description of the psychoanalytic procedure, but is clearly well aware that there are conditions in which analytic technique, designed for neurotic patients, has to be modified and the aims of analysis limited.

Jacobson, in her paper, deals specifically with the treatment of severely depressed patients, and suggests a modification of the analytic treatment aim in such patients, saying that 'mostly the therapeutic success with depressives can be gauged by their ability to remodel an unfortunate life situation which prior to analysis was bound to precipitate depressive states'

(Jacobson, 1954, p. 606). Anna Freud, discussing Stone's and Jacobson's papers, describes a case in which the aim of analysis was certainly affected by a basic deficiency in the patient's ego structure. The adolescent patient, a victim of the Nazi regime, required of the analyst that she 'offer herself in the flesh as the image of a steady, ever-present object, suitable for internalisation, so that the patient's personality could be regrouped and unified around this image' (Freud, 1954, p. 613). This was a consequence of the patient having had 'no opportunity to introject any one object sufficiently to build up inner harmony and synthesis under the guidance of a higher agency, acting as a unifying superego' (p. 613). Clearly, if such a requirement on the patient's part is recognised, the technique of the analytic work must change accordingly. Yet the question remains, Anna Freud implies, of whether the therapy is analytic or rather resembles the work of a 'preparatory phase', which would be followed by analysis proper.

It emerged from the widening-scope discussion that the aims of analysis have to be adapted to the needs and limitations of individual patients, and that analysis should not be regarded as a fixed and inflexible method to be applied indiscriminately, whatever the condition of the patient. In spite of this the American Psychoanalytic Association continued to insist on the requirement that supervised ('control') cases analysed by candidates in training at its official institutes be neurotic cases in which 'standard' technique was thought to be appropriate. A series of papers appeared at this time dealing with the traditional psychoanalytic technique and its variations as well as with comparing psychoanalysis and psychotherapy (Orr, 1954; Greenacre, 1954; Alexander, 1954a, 1954b; Weigert, 1954; Fromm-Reichmann, 1954; Rangell, 1954; Bibring, 1954; Gill, 1954). Some of the authors (Gill, Bibring, Rangell) maintained a strict definition of psycho-analysis, the aim of which was seen as the resolution of the transference neurosis. At the same time they drew attention to the problems involved in the attempt to achieve analytic aims, particularly with patients who were not 'classical neurotics'. With hindsight, it is possible to see how these authors, as well as others at that time, were trying to achieve a balance between the need, in specific cases, to modify the psychoanalytic method and aims on the one hand, and a reluctance to relax the dividing line between psychoanalysis and psychoanalytically orientated psychotherapy, on the other. This reluctance could be described as, in part at any rate, political, in that it was to some extent motivated by the reluctance of established analysts to endanger their professional status by endorsing psychotherapy, which was seen as the manipulation of transference for therapeutic ends. In contrast, other analysts (especially Alexander, Fromm-Reichmann and Weigert, who were not establishment figures) argued in the direction of de-emphasising any sharp distinction between psycho-analysis and psychoanalytically orientated psychotherapy. It is clear that the

1950s saw the beginnings of a major preoccupation – at least in the United States – with this distinction. Later in this chapter we shall comment on the significantly different situation among psychoanalysts in Britain.

What follows reflects the emergence of a variety of contradictory trends relating to the applicability and limitations of psychoanalysis – a consequence of the concern about the 'widening scope' of psychoanalysis. We can begin our account with a report of a panel on 'Goals in therapy', held at a meeting of the American Psychiatric Association in 1955 (reported by Kelman, 1956), where much attention was paid to the relativity of formulations regarding the aims of psychoanalytic therapy. In his contribution to the panel, Oskar Diethelm reiterates the view that 'dependent on the therapist's personal philosophy and his theoretical background, and on current cultural attitudes and influences, goals will be formulated differently' (Kelman, 1956, p. 4). Here Diethelm is in accord with Horney (1951), who indicated that the aims of psychoanalytic therapy depend on the analyst's *Weltanschauung*. This was an idea which was to surface again and again in various forms in mainstream psychoanalysis. He also commented on the important fact that 'goals will change during prolonged treatment and can therefore be considered only temporary, dependent on a nonpredictable future' (p. 6). It is worth noting that the need to change goals during the course of an analysis had been brought out in a paper by Maxwell Gitelson (1954) on the problem of analysing the 'normal' candidate (who is in analysis as a requirement of his analytic training). Gitelson points out that 'normality may be an adaptation appropriate to the culture, but ill-adapted to analysis'. This can make analysis extremely difficult, as the patient 'lives in terms of a facade whose structure is patterned by his environment. This provides opportunistic gratification of his instincts by virtue of their imbrication with the demands of his environment' (p. 183). It thus becomes an aim of psychoanalysis to provide an opportunity 'to test out a new reality – the analytic situation, to establish its integrity, and to prove its relevance to the basic nature of the person. In this context, and looking upon the culturally determined "normal" behaviour as itself a resistance, we may attempt to mobilise conflict made latent by the culture and thus, in the end analyse the vicissitudes of the libido itself' (p. 183).

In the 1955 panel, Nathan Ackerman remarks that 'it ought to come as no surprise that each therapist evolves a relatively personal set of criteria for the goals of therapy and the science of cure' (Kelman, 1956, p. 9). He adds, 'the goals of therapy and the connotations of cure constitute a hierarchy of meanings, which may be applied with flexibility and discrimination to a wide assortment of illnesses and psychotherapeutic undertakings. In some, it may make sense to rest content with a lesser cure; in others it is fitting and right that we aspire to a more complete and superior quality of cure' (Kelman, 1956, p. 11).

The first panel to be recorded on the goals of child analysis was held by the American Psychoanalytic Association in 1956 (reported by Bernstein, 1956). Child analysis had tended to be regarded in the past as having the same goals as adult analysis, but now emphasis was placed on the need for a careful evaluation of the structure of the child's conflicts and problems in order to decide which form of therapy would be most appropriate. Here we see the influence of increased weight being given to the current external environment and the 'external' conflicts which this might produce. The literature on child analysis had been expanding during the 1950s, and much of what was said in relation to child development was to prove relevant to the understanding of the mental functioning of the adult, and consequently for his analysis. In a consideration of the distinction between 'normal' and 'pathological' defence in the development of the child, Lampl-de Groot (1957) suggests that 'we view the neurotic defence mechanisms as pathologically exaggerated or distorted regulation and adaptation mechanisms, which in themselves belong to normal development. . . . Mental mechanisms, which may later be used as neurotic defence mechanisms in adult neuroses, are normal developmental mechanisms in early childhood, as long as they serve and promote the ego's regulative and adaptive capacities' (pp. 117, 122). She concludes that 'In analysis we should try to give the patient's ego the opportunity for abolishing the pathological, rigid employment of the mechanisms in the neurotic conflicts, and we should try to open ways for their regulative, constructive use in order to promote a harmonious afterdevelopment and unfolding of the total personality' (pp. 125–126). Lampl-de Groot's paper was thoroughly embedded in an ego-psychological point of view, and the therapeutic changes in children were seen in terms of changes in the ego's employment of its mechanisms of defence.

Ernst Kris's article, 'On some vicissitudes of insight in psychoanalysis' (1956), is a brilliant summary of the status of the ego-psychological viewpoint at that time. Kris regards the aim of gaining insight as crucial for the success of the analytic process with adults. A precondition for insight is the ability of the ego to regain the supremacy it had lost (here Kris refers in particular to the control of regression). Further, the ego needs to cultivate its self-observing function, involving the achievement of relative objectivity in the patient's perceptions about himself. (Kramer, in 1959, was to refer to the auto-analytic function of the ego.) The ego needs to gain fuller control over the discharge of affects, and to diminish acting out. As a consequence of these achievements and the gaining of insight, 'some decisive changes in self-representation, personal relations and reality testing tend particularly to develop *pari passu* with a better understanding of the individual's past' (p. 452).

In addition to the contemporary ego-psychological views, a variety of approaches, explicit and implicit, relating to aims, is further reflected in contributions by such independent thinkers as Karen Horney, Edward Glover, Thomas Szasz and Ronald Fairbairn. Horney (1951), in a paper on the aims of psychoanalytic therapy, puts forward the view that the aims of psychoanalysis were not only to achieve symptom cure but that the analyst's orientation should be towards improvement in the patient's relationships and to his discovering the nature of his personality. As she puts it, 'the aim of the analysis consists in the patient getting to know himself, how he is (current self), to make a new orientation and the finding of the true self possible (real self)' (p. 470).[2] These topics were to receive particular attention in later years in what came to be called object-relations theory, and in the work of such authors as Donald Winnicott and Heinz Kohut.

Glover's paper (1954) makes a distinction between structural changes brought about by analysis and the relief of internal dynamic stresses. He asks whether analysis 'is pursued for the purpose of bringing about structural changes or for the relief of dynamic (functional) stresses' (p. 97). Glover maintains that although the latter approach may be based on psychoanalytic understanding, it is not in itself specifically psychoanalytic. Such interventions (for the relief of 'dynamic stresses', e.g. reassurance) might function as a preparation for analysis.

Glover is concerned with underlining the situation of growing complexity which existed in the 1950s, and assesses the implications of the responses to a questionnaire which he had circulated among members of the British Society some twenty years previously. He concludes that there was 'no evidence that even an approximate consensus of opinion on therapeutic criteria has been reached. On the contrary, even if we exclude such schisms as arise from the plain abandonment of psychoanalytic principles, the tendency to fission within analytic groups in this and other countries has come to affect more and more the criteria that should govern psychoanalytic therapy' (p. 95). As Glover sees it, one of the reasons for this is 'the development of fundamental differences regarding analytical theory and aetiology' (p. 95).

These fundamental differences are reflected in a polemical attack on the Kleinian and Middle Group members of the British Society. It is worth bearing in mind that Glover, a member of the group around Anna Freud, resigned from the British Society during the 1943 Controversial Discussions (King and Steiner, 1991) as a protest against what he saw as the unacceptable Kleinian view of the time that 'no analysis could be regarded as satisfactory that did not uncover the infantile depressive position, a stage of organization which . . . is held . . . to develop during the first few

---

2 Our translation.

months of post-natal life!' (p. 95). He also expressed biting criticism of the Middle Group who, he said, 'compensate themselves for their absence of originality by extracting virtue from their eclecticism, maintaining . . . that, whether or not principles differ, scientific truth lies only in compromise' (p. 95). However, whatever Glover's motives were for writing the paper, we cannot but agree with his conclusion that empirical research is needed to eliminate from our deliberations 'the influence of a defensive, esoteric but so far unconfessed *mystique*', and that we should 'establish clinical in addition to theoretical criteria' for defining analytic treatment as opposed to psychoanalytic psychotherapy, and should also 'call for the close application of controlled research methods' (p. 100).

While the widening-scope discussions were extremely important for the development of psychoanalysis in the United States, they were not regarded as important by most British psychoanalysts (except by colleagues of Anna Freud). However, in England, a major widening-scope development occurred in Kleinian technique, in that increased attention began to be paid to the analysis of psychotic patients (see Bion, 1954; Rosenfeld, 1954; Segal, 1950). However, apart from the fact that psychotic patients were not always put on the couch, the technique of interpretation and the aims of analysis remained essentially the same as for non-psychotic patients. There was no question of regarding the analysis of psychotic or borderline patients as psychotherapy. In the Middle Group, analysts like Winnicott (1954), Balint (1952) and Margaret Little (1958) advocated modifications of psychoanalytic technique, but here again, this was generally accepted as being analysis rather than psychotherapy. In the British Society candidates of all groups were often confronted with atypical or borderline patients for their supervised (control) cases. Psychotherapy was seen as being carried out by therapists not trained in the British Society, or by analysts who saw their patients less than four or five times a week.

We end this chapter with a fairly full account of papers by Szasz and Fairbairn. Szasz presents a remarkably comprehensive discussion of the aims of psychoanalysis in a paper 'On the theory of psychoanalytic treatment' (1957). He is highly critical of the influence of the medical model on psychoanalytic technique, resulting in psychoanalysis being primarily seen as a 'treatment', and indicates his full agreement with Freud in turning from the goal of curing the patient to the aim of trying to understand better the nature of what the patient produced – 'the goal of helping the patient became subsidiary to the goal of scientific understanding' (p. 167). Szasz elaborates a very persuasive parallel between analytic technique and the aims and rules of chess in the following way:

1 Both are restricted to those who know how to play the game.

2 Both can be described in terms of a set of rules which, in their elementary components, do not appear very complicated.

3 The latitude within the rules in both is determined by what the participants bring to the situation.

4 While the rules are set and predetermined, the game proceeds in such a way that each player influences the other continuously.

5 The notions of 'rigidity' and 'flexibility' are not relevant to the rules of both, since we take for granted that the participants agree to abide by the rules as a matter of convention.

6 In all situations characterised by rules, the rules structure the situation, but the participants determine the complexity and richness which may develop therein.

7 The final goals are given and are not a matter of choice for the participants.

Szasz finds himself at one with Freud in viewing analysis as a *method* of investigation; however, he sees it as being like chess, in that it is a method which has a variety of possible technical 'moves' allowed by the rules, and it is these which determine the aims of analysis. The rules of the game and its aim are *complementary concepts*, and

> given a certain set of rules for the technique of psychoanalysis, we shall have to ask not what the analyst's or the patient's aims or aspirations are, but what *aim* may have been 'built into' the therapeutic procedures by its very operations.
>
> (1957, p. 172)

Szasz differentiates *intermediary* goals from a *final* goal. It is interesting to read what he says in this connection:

> Since there is general agreement that there is something inherently *unending* about analysis as a process (not as a situation), would it not be helpful if the final goal of treatment were formulated so that it were to be consistent with this viewpoint? In accord with the foregoing considerations, I believe that the final goal of analysis should be stated neither in the frame of reference of technique, nor in that of social or interpersonal adaptation, but rather in general terms which pertain to the person's (ego's) orientation to his past and present inner life (objects) as well as to his outside life experiences. How can we describe this final state and do justice to all the requirements mentioned? The answer to this question may be found in Freud's writings, although he did not formulate it as explicitly as I will state it now. According to this view the final goal of psychoanalytic treatment is the establishment of a never-ending ever-

deepening *scientific attitude* in the patient towards those segments of his life which constitute the sphere of psychoanalysis. The sphere of analysis . . . consists of man's life history, his internal objects, and his ever-changing life experiences. . . . It must be remembered that a definition of the final goal of analysis, as stated above, does *not* supersede the several intermediary goals, described by Freud and others. Rather, the concept of the final goal must be *added* to some of our previous concepts in order to arrive at a more comprehensive theoretical synthesis of what constitutes analytic treatment.

(1957, p. 176)

Following Waelder (1936), Szasz regards the *scientific attitude* referred to above as 'the *ability to differentiate between the possible and the real*' (p. 176). The goal of 'helping the patient' and that of the patient's adopting a progressively more scientific attitude towards himself and his relationships with others are not two separate processes but 'are complementary and not mutually exclusive'.

Szasz adheres firmly to the view that analysis, like chess, is a procedure or technique which has many *intermediate* possibilities built into it. Its rules and thus its aims are defined and should not be modified to suit any particular patient, although the path the process takes may differ markedly from one patient to another. Linked with this is his disapproval of the word 'treatment' as applied to psychoanalysis, which

ordinarily refers to the activity of but one person in a situation or interaction with another person (or persons); whereas in psychoanalysis, the proper meaning of 'treatment' depends on the activity of both analyst and analysand and, accordingly, in this context it refers to a process which *includes* and abstracts the activities of the participants in it.

(1957, p. 178)

In spite of the elegance of Szasz's paper, it did not find approval everywhere. It prompted Ronald Fairbairn, one of the most distinguished exponents of the British object-relations school,[3] to express his disagreement with some of Szasz's views in a paper entitled 'On the nature and aims of psychoanalytical treatment' (1958). He is critical, among other things, of the view that psychoanalysis is not a form of treatment 'since the operative motive in the

---

3 Fairbairn, in his *Object Relations Theory of the Personality* (1954), maintained that the ego was the source of libido which was object-seeking rather than pleasure-seeking. Aggression was seen as a reaction to frustration, and consequently the notion of an id was unnecessary, and could be replaced by the idea of a 'libidinal' and an 'anti-libidinal' ego. The role of the interaction between the self and external objects was accorded great importance.

patient is . . . a desire to obtain relief from symptoms . . . in accepting a patient for psychoanalytical treatment, the analyst implicitly adopts a therapeutic aim' (pp. 376–377). Fairbairn comments,

> In general, I cannot help feeling that any tendency to adhere with pronounced rigidity to the details of the classic psychoanalytic technique, as standardised by Freud more than half a century ago, is liable to defensive exploitation, however unconscious this may be, in the interests of the analyst and at the expense of the patient; and certainly any tendency to treat the classic technique as sacrosanct raises the suspicion that an element of such a defensive exploitation is at work. Further, it seems to me that a complete stultification of the therapeutic aim is involved in any demand, whether explicit or implicit, that the patient must conform to the nature of the therapeutic method rather than that the method must conform to the requirement of the patient.
>
> (1958, pp. 378–379)

In elaborating his view of the therapeutic process, Fairbairn says that 'the really decisive factor is the relationship of the patient to the analyst, and it is upon this relationship that the other factors . . . depend not only for their effectiveness, but for their very existence, since in the absence of a therapeutic relationship with the analyst they do not occur. . . . It should be added that what I understand by "the relationship between the patient and the analyst" is not just the relationship involved in the transference, but the total relationship existing between the patient and the analyst as persons' (p. 379). The chief aim of psychoanalytic treatment is

> to promote a maximum 'synthesis' of the structures into which the original ego has been split, in the setting of a therapeutic relationship with the analyst. Involved in the achievement of this aim are two further aims, viz. (a) a maximum reduction of persisting infantile dependence, and (b) a maximum reduction of that hatred of the libidinal object which, according to my theory, is ultimately responsible for the original splitting of the ego. . . . [In addition] it becomes still another aim of psychoanalytic treatment to effect breaches of the closed system which constitutes the patient's inner world, and thus to make this world accessible to the influence of outer reality.
>
> (1958, p. 380)

He concludes with a striking comment on how psychoanalytic treatment works, and to what purpose.

> Psychoanalytic treatment resolves itself into a struggle on the part of the patient to press-gang his relationship with the analyst into the

closed system of the inner world through the agency of transference, and a determination on the part of the analyst to effect a breach in this closed system and to provide conditions under which, in the setting of a therapeutic relationship, the patient may be induced to accept the open system of outer reality.

(1958, p. 385)

We cannot leave the 1950s without reference to the monograph by Marie Jahoda on *Current Concepts of Positive Mental Health* (1958). In this work, produced for the Joint Commission on Mental Illness and Health in the United States, Jahoda reviews the extensive literature on mental health and illness, including significant psychoanalytic contributions. She categorises and clarifies the psychological meaning of the various criteria put forward for assessing mental health (see a similar comprehensive attempt made much later by McGlashan and Miller, 1982). Jahoda groups the criteria under the headings of 'attitudes towards the self', 'growth, development, and self-actualization', 'integration', 'reality-orientation', 'autonomy', 'perception of reality' and 'environmental mastery'. In agreement with Hartmann (1939b), she points out that there are many diverse types of person who can be regarded as healthy, and concludes that it is necessary to adopt a 'multiple criterion' approach to the assessment of mental health. Quite different criteria may apply to different people, and no single criterion is adequate for the assessment of mental health. Jahoda then points to what she calls the 'value dilemma'.

Different persons will prefer different values and the criteria discussed here have differing relations to these values. A *prima facie* case could be made, for example, that meeting the requirements of the situation is more closely related to the maintenance of the *status quo* or to conformity than to creativity; or that the criterion of adaptation may automatically discriminate in favour of the economically secure who are in a better position to modify their environment than are those who live in less privileged circumstances. . . . How culture or social class bound is the value orientation of those who have suggested the criteria? Would people living in an Oriental civilization have considered contemplation and detachment as suitable criteria? Would the mental health label be more appropriately attached to self-assertive aggressiveness, to fit dominant values in the working class in Western civilizations?

(1958, pp. 77–78)

Wallerstein has remarked that Jahoda's conceptions of mental health and normality have become benchmarks against which to measure therapeutic achievements, given all of the cultural and value contextualisation with

68

which we have to surround conceptions of health and normality (personal communication).

To conclude . . .

While little new was explicitly said in regard to psychoanalytic aims during the 1950s, important developments were beginning to take shape. The widening-scope discussions reflected an awareness that psychoanalytic technique had to be flexible and needed to be modified in order to fit the analytic needs of individual patients. In turn, this prompted reactions of two different sorts. On the one hand, there was a rigidifying of technique by an insistence on the need for a 'standard' procedure, capable of being modified only temporarily by so-called 'parameters' (Eissler, 1953). On the other hand, ego psychology began to take notice of differences in the development and structure of the ego, and attempted to view non-neurotic pathology in terms of ego functioning. Consequently the outcome of the psychoanalytic treatment was considered in terms of structural changes in the ego. In addition to these developments in the United States, formulations in terms of object relationships were increasingly finding their way into the literature on psychoanalytic theory and practice. As Loewald, in an excellent article, 'On the therapeutic action of psychoanalysis' (1960), put it: 'While the fact of an object relationship between patient and analyst is taken for granted, classical formulations concerning therapeutic action and concerning the role of the analyst in the analytic relationship do not reflect our present understanding of the dynamic organisation of the psychic apparatus' (1960 [1980], p. 222).

The tendencies evident in the 1950s continued into the next decade as conceptual tensions which would eventually crystallise into definite schools within the psychoanalytic movement.

6

Heightening tensions

In the 1950s psychoanalytic writers had begun to show greater independence of thought, adhering less to previously accepted conceptualisations. At the same time a reaction to this tendency occurred, with a concomitant tendency towards maintaining analytic rigidity. The discussion of aims moved in the direction of focusing on intrapsychic modifications brought about by analysis, changes in the individual's relation to his personal environment having been seen in terms of such modifications. While there was an awareness of the need for greater flexibility of approach in the therapy of patients who were not suffering from neurosis, the view of what the analytic method was remained relatively rigid, particularly in the United States; in other words, there was a 'standard technique', and variations in that technique tended to be seen as 'deviations' from what was regarded as proper analytic practice. On the other hand, statements by such authors as Fairbairn (1958) pointed to the need for a greater flexibility in what should be regarded as 'proper' analysis. Fairbairn's comment that 'a complete stultification of the therapeutic aim is involved in any demand, whether explicit or implicit, that the patient must conform to the nature of the therapeutic method rather than that the method must conform to the requirement of the patient' (1958, p. 379) could have been a reaction both to the rigidity of 'classical' analysis and to the technique advocated by the followers of Melanie Klein. However, more attention now began to be paid to the nature of the therapeutic factors which bring about intrapsychic change through analysis, with closer links being forged between psychoanalytic metapsychology and the theory of psychoanalytic therapy. Thus Hans Loewald (1960) links the analytic process and ego development, which he sees as

a process of increasingly higher integration and differentiation of the psychic apparatus. . . . An analysis can be characterised, from this standpoint, as a period or periods of induced ego disorganisation and

reorganisation . . . [it is] an intervention designed to set ego development in motion, be it from a point of relative arrest, or to promote
what we conceive of as a healthier direction and/or compre-
hensiveness of such development. . . . [The process of change is] set
in motion not simply by the technical skill of the analyst, but by the
fact that the analyst makes himself available for the development of a
new 'object-relationship' between the patient and the analyst. . . .
We know from analytic as well as from life experience that new
spurts of self-development may be intimately connected with such
'regressive' rediscoveries of oneself as may occur through the
establishment of new object-relationships . . . the opportunity they
offer for rediscovery of the early paths of the development of object-
relations, leading to a new way of relating to objects as well as of
being and relating to oneself.

(Loewald, 1960 [1980], pp. 224–225)[1]

The awareness that such changes could not always be brought about
during the course of the analytic work led to a more realistic appreciation
of the limitations of the method, and therefore to more understanding of
the need to be less ambitious in regard to what analysis could and could not
achieve in individual cases. The impetus towards a greater realism during
the 1960s was strengthened by two outstanding books on psychoanalytic
technique, Leo Stone's *The Psychoanalytic Situation* (1961), and Ralph
Greenson's *The Technique and Practice of Psychoanalysis* (1967).

The 1960s was an important decade in the development of psychoanalysis. In Britain, sufficient time had elapsed since the Controversial
Discussions of the early 1940s (King and Steiner, 1991) for constructive
dialogue to start between the three groups in the British Society. Attempts

---

1 Loewald's discussion is based on his comprehensive theoretical model of intrapsychic
   structure and its functioning, the aim of psychoanalytic therapy being formulated in
   terms of ongoing changes in the structure of the psychic apparatus. His views may, at
   first sight, resemble those of Franz Alexander who, following his early paper 'A
   metapsychological description of the process of cure' (1925), developed more fully
   the ideas put forward there after his founding of the Chicago Institute in 1932. The
   best known of these ideas was the concept of the 'corrective emotional experience'
   in which the analyst attempted to correct the patient's superego through the
   transference, by adopting a new superego stance, one which was different from that
   of the patient's own superego. The intention of the analyst in this technique was
   'actively' (through intentional changes in the analyst's attitude) to expose the patient
   to differences between the original conflict situation and the current analytic situation
   (Alexander and French, 1946). This approach has generally been regarded as manipu-
   lative and non-analytic. Loewald's approach, on the other hand, is non-manipulative
   and analytic.

71

began to be made by an increasing number of analysts to understand and to look for the value of ideas put forward by members of other groups. At the same time there was still an unwillingness among many to give up entrenched group positions; and while the discussion of clinical material tended to lead to the discovery of common ground, theoretical 'deviations' were, on the whole, looked at askance. A similar tension was noticeable in the United States, where, although new ideas were being put forward, American psychoanalysis was still heavily controlled by the ego-psychological establishment. We can see this, for example, in the lack of recognition afforded at the time to the work of such analysts as Loewald, who was only later to be appropriately recognised as a major contributor. While the 1960s were productive years, tension between the proponents of different views was still high, and the reader may well feel that this tension is apparent in the structure of this chapter. It has been difficult to characterise a major trend in this decade except (as we found after writing this chapter) by conveying a sense of conflict and the resulting tension through our selection of material.

It is significant that in 1964 the American Psychoanalytic Association decided to hold a panel on 'Limitations of psychoanalysis' (reported by Gray, 1965). There Wallerstein presented his paper on 'The goals of psychoanalysis' (1965), which is regarded as a milestone in the attempt to organise and formalise the concept of analytic aims. His paper is subtitled 'a survey of analytic viewpoints', and Wallerstein does indeed present a comprehensive historical survey. The paper is, incidentally, an excellent example of the use of historical research to produce a model of the way in which analytic aims can be discussed and organised. His overview results in a division of analytic aims into different levels or categories, and he links changes in the conceptualisation of aims with external factors, including modifications which have occurred in the theoretical climate of psychoanalysis.

Wallerstein's paper begins with the statement: 'A discussion of the limitations of psychoanalysis as a treatment modality necessarily raises the question of the ideal and of the practical goals of psychoanalytic treatment against which its inevitable shortcomings are to be measured.' In the literature on goals, distinctions have been made between formulations which are, in his view, distinctions which stress *idealised* goals and those which refer to *attainable* goals. He says:

> I wish to focus in more explicit fashion on the question of goals per se, from the standpoint of three major polarities, each of which at first glance seems to pose a paradox, or at least a complementarity of viewpoints. The first seeming paradox is that between goallessness (or desirelessness) as a technical tool marking the proper therapeutic posture of analytic work and the fact that psychoanalysis differentiates

itself from all other psychotherapies, analytically oriented or not, by positing the most ambitious and far-reaching goals in terms of the possibilities of fundamental personality reorganisation.

(1965, p. 749)

The second major polarity is the distinction between 'the goals of psychoanalysis that are related to the outcomes striven for and the goals of psychoanalysis that are set in terms of the analytic process as an instrument to bring about those changes'. *Outcome* goals are conceived in terms of observable behaviour and changes in relationships, while *process* goals relate to the *intermediate* changes brought about during analysis. Wallerstein says, after his review of process and outcome goals as they are reflected in the literature, that there is a tacit assumption

> that the two develop together and in appropriate correspondence to each other – that is, that the achievement of analytic insights in the process of making the unconscious conscious is the constant and the necessary and the (implicitly) sufficient concomitant of the achievement of the outcome goals, to be able to love and to work. . . . Yet we know, too, that unhappily this does not always follow.

(1965, p. 763)

However, Wallerstein's summary of his position in regard to this second polarity provides another slant. He says it is 'the distinction between outcome goals of analytic therapy conceptualised in terms of observable behaviour and relationship changes and the process goals of analytic therapy conceptualised in metapsychological explanatory terms that posit at least implicitly a theory of therapy, of how analysis brings about change and reaches its outcome goals' (p. 768).

The third polarity used in the assessment of the relevant literature is 'the oscillating distinction between the more limited and the more ambitious, the more pessimistic and the more optimistic view of how much of this sought-for change can actually be accomplished within the limits of human analytic endeavour' (p. 768).

In his paper on 'Psychoanalysis: reflections and comments', Glueck (1960), in some ways foreshadowing Wallerstein's formulations (1965), makes a distinction between *proximate* and *ultimate* goals. He is worth quoting *in extenso*.

> We have been in the habit of distinguishing between a psychoanalytic therapy and all other forms of psychotherapy, by suggesting, indeed sometimes insisting, with quite an unjustifiable arrogance, that in all nonpsychoanalytic psychotherapies we are content to relieve the patient of his symptoms, whereas in a psychoanalysis the basic object

of this experience is to rid the patient of his need to generate symptoms. This is true, but not entirely so, and only a fool would underestimate too greatly the importance to the patient to be rid of his symptoms. Leaving aside for the moment the primary obligation of the physician to relieve suffering, I have come to view the goals and objectives of a psychoanalytic therapy in the following manner.

I differentiate to begin with between proximate goals near at hand and . . . distant or ultimate goals. As to these latter ultimate goals, we aim firstly to help the patient gain a deeper and broader self knowledge . . . which usually helps to reduce to a minimum the common human tendency to ambivalency. The emergence of this type of insight has been designated as a 'leap' from darkness to light. It illuminates, sometimes with dramatic suddenness, things which have been obscure and unrecognisable before. These flashes of insight help the patient to integrate feelings and events of which he might have already been more or less aware, but only as disparate, unrelated and meaningless parts of wholes.

Secondly, a well conducted psychoanalytic therapy aims to help the patient gain a more complete self realisation and to become an individual in his own right, liberated as far as possible from inhibiting fears and anxieties which render difficult or impossible the facing of life's issues honestly and courageously. One should gain, in the course of a psychoanalysis, the firm conviction that no-one who is afraid to look at himself honestly and to understand himself can possibly achieve a competent, courageous and creative life. The achievement of a firm and secure capacity for self realisation should render unnecessary the resort to affectations of any sort or to confusing, hampering and unreasonable defensive manoeuvres.

The third major goal which psychoanalytic therapy would aim to achieve is a satisfying, syntonic self acceptance, the best that is possible for a given individual under the circumstances of his life.

These three goals of self understanding, self realisation and self acceptance are indispensable to the achievement of a competence for self direction. The attainment of them naturally does not carry with it any sense of finality or completeness. We know that the living human organism is never a finished product, and that growth and expansiveness of the 'self' can go on as long as life lasts, if no serious obstacles stand in its way.

In addition to these ultimate goals mentioned above, many proximate or immediate goals are naturally achieved also in a well conducted psychoanalytic therapy, beneficial to the patient and highly rewarding to the physician. But it is my firm opinion that no psychoanalysis is really ever finished. No matter how much time is consumed by a particular psychoanalytic experience, it can at best deal only with a sampling of the great number, variety and complexity of issues that enter into the shaping of a human life. But enough of a sampling it must be which would enable the patient or student to experience something of the nature and the strength of the dynamisms of unconscious motivation; something of the interplay of emotion in the transference situation; a sampling of the manner by which anxiety is generated and what its relation is to symptom formation and to the need it creates for symptoms as palliatives against the distresses of anxiety. Only when one succeeds in achieving the goals so far discussed, can one truly claim that important distinction for psychoanalytic therapy, namely that it aims to abolish the need for symptom formation.

(1960, pp. 134–135)

The delineation of 'levels of aim' by such authors as Glueck and Wallerstein raises again issues of normality and mental health. Two papers from Europe are concerned with this topic. The first is by E.E. Krapf of Geneva (1961), who discusses in detail the problems surrounding the concepts of normality and health. He cites the well-known distinctions between 'statistical normality' and 'normative normality', the latter being 'that which is such as it *should* be'. Although there are difficulties inherent in the concept of normality, he concludes that it is possible to arrive at a psychoanalytic definition of mental health. 'If we believe that the real cure of a psychopathological case is not confined to the disappearance of the symptoms, but includes the attainment of a permanent stabilisation of the personality, it is impossible to be satisfied with the concept which is based only on static and phenomenological characteristics' (p. 441).

Two essential criteria for mental health are elaborated by Krapf. These are *reasonableness* and *balance*. Reasonableness means the predominance of the ego over the id, characterised by 'reason and circumspection'. Balance is important because 'too great a predominance of the reasonable ego is hardly more healthy than a complete domination of the id'. In this he is at one with Hartmann (1939a), who had put forward the view that 'a healthy ego should be capable of making use of the system of rational control and, at the same time, of recognising the irrational nature of other mental activities'. In Krapf's view the ego needs 'a good orientation towards the ideal. . . . The quality of the orientation towards the ideal depends above all upon the values which the cultural environment "proposes" to the person. . . . The "proposers" are, in the first place, the parents, but also the other members of the family and the social and cultural environment in general' (1961, p. 442).

Krapf makes a nice point when he remarks that children and adolescents may not possess the reasonable equilibrium or 'balance' which would characterise mental health in adults. While their behaviour might look pathological, they need not be characterised as ill. This is because they may be showing the effects of regression producing imbalance or (as in adolescence), the manifestations of incomplete progression. 'This permits us', he says, 'to define the mental health of a young person in very precise terms: we consider a developing person when he is not hampered in his progression and is therefore able to complete it as his biological growth proceeds' (p. 443). Here Krapf's statement fits precisely with Anna Freud's view that the aim of child analysis is to restore the child to the path of normal development (1965).

He concludes that it is correct to criticise those 'who (generally without knowing it) introduce their own cultural values into concepts of mental health which are presented as universally valid. But the psychoanalytic concept is not open to this objection, for it rests upon the person's capacity to choose between modifying his behaviour and his environment' (p. 444). Above all, the individual's mental health is characterised by his capacity for *flexible adaptation*, which results in 'the setting-up of an equilibrium of the psyche with reason and ego predominating' (p. 444).

While there is much to be said for Krapf's ideas, his argument that the psychoanalytic concept of mental health is not influenced by the analyst's cultural values is manifestly incorrect. The very emphasis placed by Krapf on the person's capacity to choose between modifying his behaviour and his environment introduces (perhaps without knowing it) the values of Western civilisation, in which freedom of choice is highly regarded.

The second paper from Europe, 'The aims of psychoanalytical treatment' by Donald Winnicott (1962), is concerned with the same topic as Krapf, less directly but more simply. Winnicott, a prominent member of the Independent Group in the British Society, approaches the issue in a typical Winnicottian fashion: 'In doing psychoanalysis I aim at:

Keeping alive
Keeping well
Keeping awake

Winnicott considers how the *analyst* functions when with a patient, and discusses the different way he approaches the situation when using 'standard technique' and when 'modified analysis'. His emphasis in regard to aims is, however, not only on processes in the analyst, but also on changes in the patient's ego from a developmental point of view, i.e., a change from the state in which 'growth and emotional development [had] become held up in the original situation'. He emphasises the implicit aim of developing what he speaks of in other contexts as the 'true self' ('The theory of the parent–infant relationship', 1960a, and 'Ego distortion in terms of true and false self', 1960b). Winnicott's concept of the false self has been described as follows: 'The maturational processes can be by-passed by a series of identifications, so that what shows clinically is a false, acting self, a copy of someone perhaps; and what could be called a true or essential self becomes hidden, and becomes deprived of living experience' (Khan *et al.*, 1974, p. 637). For Winnicott, progress in analysis is connected with the diminution of false-self tendencies, with ego integration and the patient's growing ability to gather all things into the area of his personal control. The patient should feel freer, even if not free of symptoms. Winnicott comments,

> In my opinion our aims in the practice of the standard technique are not altered if it happens that we interpret mental mechanisms which belong to the psychotic types of disorder and to primitive stages in the emotional stages of the individual. If our aim continues to be to verbalise the nascent conscious in terms of the transference, then we are practising analysis; if not, then we are analysts practising something else that we deem to be appropriate to the occasion. And why not?
>
> (1962, pp. 169–170)

Winnicott's last point raises again the issue of whether a necessary departure from 'standard' technique is or is not analysis. His idea that analysis is restricted in its primary aim to 'verbalise the nascent conscious in terms of the transference' is, in our view, too narrow a definition of analysis.

A concept not far removed from Winnicott's notion of the 'true self' was put forward by Bernard Robbins in the USA, in a paper on 'The process of cure in psychotherapy' (1960). There he formulated the aims of psychoanalysis in terms of 'freedom', as a new concept of cure. 'Freedom' is seen as a composite of intrapsychic and social factors:

> What then, we may ask, is freedom? What is cure? It is the recognition of all necessities, both internal and external, personal and social, and the recognition of the interrelationship and interdependence of the two. Cure is not, as Freud would have us believe, the obliteration of personal necessity in the interest of 'conformation or adjustment to society'; or, as others hold, the aggrandizement of personal necessities free of external pressure or forces.
>
> In my opinion, freedom of the individual, cure, is (1) the recognition of personal necessities and their compatibility with one another, (2) their compatibility with the necessities of others and (3) the possession of means and tools for their fulfilment. This represents our therapeutic goal. This, too, is our social goal.
>
> (1960, pp. 98–99)

While Robbins emphasises the interdependence of personal and social factors, he, together with Krapf and Winnicott, implicitly raises the issue of the attainment of increased autonomy as an aim of analysis. Some years earlier, David Rapaport, writing on the theory of ego autonomy (1958), had elaborated on Hartmann's (1939b) conception of autonomy by differentiating between two relative autonomies, i.e., autonomy from the drives, and autonomy from the external world. Autonomy – always relative – means freedom from enslavement either to the drives or to the demands of the external world. Later, Sandler and Joffe (1967) extended Hartmann's and Rapaport's concept of autonomy to include autonomy from the superego, and suggested that it would be more appropriate to speak of one autonomy rather than two or three.

Increased autonomy from the environment is considered by Gitelson (1962) as a significant curative factor in psychoanalysis. This ties in well with Winnicott's notion of the 'true self' (which is less orientated towards external objects than the 'false self'), with Krapf's emphasis on 'reasonableness' and 'balance' and with Robbins's concept of 'freedom'. Such personality qualities of a rather general nature appear to have replaced more strictly metapsychological formulations, and perhaps we see here an attempt to turn to formulations in everyday language in order to be in line with the developing pragmatism of the time; but this replacement does not solve the problem of conceptualising outcome (and the limitations of analysis) more precisely.

Like Winnicott, Elizabeth Zetzel (in a panel reported by Altman, 1964) saw aims in terms of development. At the panel she read a paper on 'The theory of therapy in relation to a developmental model of the psychic apparatus' (Zetzel, 1965). She draws a parallel between developmental processes and the ways in which psychic change is brought about by analysis. She believes that the gap between Hartmann's ego-psychological concept of secondary autonomy of the ego and the increasing emphasis on early object relationships could be narrowed by using a developmental model which attributes importance to the major ego functions, and the way they arose in the early mother–child relationship. Psychoanalysis requires motivation towards a progressive developmental goal, and this involves a necessary step backward, i.e., regression. Thus 'our developmental hypothesis includes by definition both progressive and regressive potentialities at all times'(1965, p. 40). Although treatment is often defined as a modified repetition of original development with a new and better resolution, Zetzel insists that a satisfactory termination of a successful analysis implies achieving the developmental steps of separation and independence. These occur through the mature acceptance of realistic limitations in regard to analysis and the analyst, and consequently in regard to the patient's optimal capacity for future achievements.[2] However, no analysis, however successful, is ever conclusively terminated.

An interesting aspect of this panel, and another (Pfeffer, 1963a), held at meetings of The American Psychoanalytic Association, is the emphasis on qualities in the patient required for a successful analysis. Thus Greenson (reported by Altman), certainly with his tongue in his cheek, gives the following extensive account of qualities analysis requires from the patient.

> First of all, the patient must have the ability to maintain contact with reality and also be able to give it up partially and temporarily. He must be able to oscillate between secondary and primary process thinking. We expect him to communicate in words, to drift, and yet he must remain comprehensible to us. We ask of him that he listen and try to understand our interventions and yet associate freely to what we have said. No matter how far he may have regressed in the hour, we expect him to be able to resume his reasonable ego functions at the end of the session. He must suffer and want to change. The wish to understand oneself is not sufficient for psychoanalysis. He must be willing to endure the deprivations of the analytic situation, the frustrations, humiliations, etc. Ultimately he must be willing to renounce the special gratifications that arise in the course of analytic therapy. The patient must be willing to forgo quick results and devote himself to long-range goals. He must be able to bear uncertainty, anxiety, and depression, and report them intelligibly without resorting to ordinary social censorship or flight into health. The patient must be willing to try to understand the analyst's communications, and eventually he must dare to risk reacting or acting in a new way. He must be able to work with the analyst, even though he may have intense feelings of love or hatred, and at the end of the hour he must be able to drive home without killing anybody. It takes a relatively healthy patient to meet these requirements!
>
> (Altman, 1964, pp. 628–629)

Indeed, we may well ask how many of our patients fulfil all or most of these requirements? Would those who do actually require analysis? What would

---

2 Gitelson (1962) had anticipated the later intense interest in the parallel between the therapeutic process and the development of the child. He pointed out that, as we come to know more about development, so we can equally know more about change in the course of analysis. He says, 'what happens "normally" in the psychoanalytic situation is comparable to the course of events under more or less normal circumstances in the developmental situation in which the child finds himself on the road to more or less non-neurotic autonomous adulthood' (p. 196).

be the aim of their treatment? Would those who are attending for analysis, but do not possess all these requirements, actually be in analysis? And what are the analytic aims in patients who are not 'relatively healthy'?

Of the greatest significance for a realistic conception of 'necessary qualities' and consequently for analytic aims is the consideration of criteria for the termination of an analysis. These had been discussed in earlier years (e.g. in the series of papers presented to the British Society in 1949 —see Chapter 4), but now they were being looked at more systematically. In a panel on 'Problems of termination in the analysis of adults' (reported by Firestein, 1969) analysts who had interviewed colleagues about the termination phase reported on their findings. Among the usual criteria listed, emphasis was placed on the need for recognition by the patient of the limitations to what therapy could achieve in his case. Included among limiting factors were the characteristics of important objects in the patient's current life. Some analysts felt that the criteria for termination were satisfied only by a minority of patients. A critical test of successful completion occurs when the patient is confronted with an unexpected disturbing experience and deals with it in a realistic rather than an infantile manner. In the panel discussion Firestein stressed the influence of the analyst's working concept of 'mental health', and pointed out that the desire for a perfect result may reflect a countertransference wish. It was said that it might be more useful to think of the termination of the analysis as an interruption, and that every analysis is fundamentally interminable, a view which had frequently been expressed in the 1960s, e.g. by Grotjahn (1964), who writes of the patient's need for an indefinite continuation of his analysis through self-analysis or through analytic interviews with his former or a new analyst ('open-end' technique). This view was endorsed in this panel discussion by Helene Deutsch, who also referred to the 'open-door' policy. In this regard Zetzel remarked that no analysis is successfully terminated unless the patient feels free to return in case of further trouble.[3]

Interestingly, as early as 1960, Robert Waelder, in his *Basic Theory of Psychoanalysis* (1960), had commented on the limitations of psychoanalysis, and his remarks at that time are very much to the point.

> If one sets as [the] goal of an analysis the complete understanding of a person's psychic life, both normal and pathological, and a complete

---

[3] Leo Stone (1961) considered that the transference is never completely resolved, and says, 'I use the term "minimisation of the transference(s)", because I have considerable scepticism regarding the likelihood of complete dissolution or extinction of the transference' (p. 70). Willi Hoffer (personal communication to J.S.) once said 'Analyses are never completed, only interrupted'.

reconstruction of the development of his personality, then an analysis can never be complete. This is all the more so as life goes on during the analytic treatment and new experience accumulates daily that has not been fully evaluated consciously.

But analysis is interminable only as long as we think of scientific completion. As far as the needs of therapy are concerned, the goals of a complete analysis are much more modest (although still ambitious enough). An analysis is complete from a therapeutic point of view if the pathological structures have been fully understood, both dynamically and genetically, and if this investigation has been extended, beyond the directly pathological traits, to a surrounding area of psychic structure likely to be related with them, or interfering with a viable solution of the underlying conflicts; if all this has been worked through with the patient in many manifestations time and again; and if the psychopathology has thereby disappeared or has been rendered controllable.

These goals are achievable, and are being achieved, in any fully satisfactory analysis, and in this sense a complete analysis is possible and is often the actual goal of analytic work.

It is an altogether different question, however, when an analytic treatment *should* be terminated because this point does not necessarily coincide with completion. Some cases cannot, and others need not, be completed. Regardless of completion, an analysis should be *terminated* when one has reached the *point of diminishing returns*, i.e., when further results which can be reasonably anticipated do not seem to justify the further time and effort which would have to be expended. That is a matter of judgement; it involves many factors.

(1960, pp. 242–243)

To conclude . . .

Looking back over the 1960s, it is apparent that the psychoanalytic views of that decade were characterised by the co-existence of remarkably contradictory points of view. In the analytic literature there is a persisting idealisation of analysis as a therapeutic method, one which can be extended to conditions other than neurosis. At the same time, probably because of the growing realisation of the difficulty in achieving a full and satisfactory termination of analysis, a realistic appreciation of limitations of what analysis could achieve was increasingly evident. Throughout the 1960s the aims of psychoanalysis were seen more clearly as specific aims for specific patients, taking their psychic structure and characterological limitations into account. The general statements of aims were more often related to questions of termination, and the criteria upon which an analysis could be judged satisfactory were listed in more detail than in the past; and it is possible to see the growing appreciation of the importance of the patient's relations to the objects of his social environment.

The particular concerns, especially in the late 1960s, about what psychoanalysis can or cannot achieve, reflect an underlying tension in American psychoanalysis in relation to 'classical' or 'standard' analysis. On the one hand, there were the professional requirements of adherence to the 'party line' of the ego-psychological establishment; on the other hand, the gap between what was feasible and what was ideal had grown, so that psychoanalytic practice did not always correspond to 'official' requirements. This tension cannot be divorced from the profound socio-cultural changes of the time. The 'American dream' was being eroded by widespread feelings of disillusionment related, for example, to the assassination of John F. Kennedy, involvement in the Vietnam War and the revolt of students against the Establishment, which was influenced by the students' movement which had begun in Europe and the events of May 1968. Psychiatry and notions of mental health and illness were profoundly affected, and discontent with orthodox psychiatry showed itself in the new ideas and practices advocated by the 'anti-psychiatry' movement. The psychoanalytic community in the United States, in its turn, was certainly not immune to these tensions and influences, and in addition was affected by the diminished influence of the first generation of immigrants who had been trained and had practised in Europe, and by the fact that the philosophical and scientific underpinnings of psychoanalysis were being increasingly and critically discussed in academic circles.

All of this provided a fertile ground for the blossoming of new approaches to psychoanalytic theory and technique in the next decades. Apart from the continuing interest in object relationships in British psychoanalysis, the new theoretical frameworks being elaborated in the United States by such authors as Edith Jacobson, Margaret Mahler, Heinz Kohut and Otto Kernberg were beginning to play a significant role.

7

The 1970s and the flowering of pluralism

Earlier we referred to the fact that since the 1940s ego psychology had dominated the psychoanalytic scene in the United States. Heinz Hartmann, Ernst Kris and Rudolph Loewenstein, all members of the New York Psychoanalytic Society, had been undisputed leaders whose followers exercised an overwhelming influence through the American Psychoanalytic Association. For an analyst to progress in his training, to gain membership in the American Association, and to become a training analyst charged with conducting the analysis and supervision of analytic candidates, it had for many years been necessary to be 'classical' and to have the ego-psychological orientation laid down by the 'establishment'. As we have seen, being 'classical' meant accepting the view that psychoanalysis was the appropriate treatment only for patients with neuroses, whose pathology was rooted in the Oedipal phase, and who consequently had the so-called infantile neurosis which was repeated in later life, and which would show itself in the transference in the form of a transference neurosis. The aim of treatment involved the 'resolution of this transference neurosis'. Alongside the awareness of the widening scope of psychoanalysis, there was among many a general feeling that cases which did not conform to the strict diagnosis of neurosis were not really suitable for 'standard' psychoanalytic treatment. Nevertheless, such cases, including cases of character disturbance and borderline personality disorder, were in fact being treated psychoanalytically more frequently. Commenting on this, Lipton asked whether we see a real widening scope of analysis or whether the situation is simply that more and more treatments were being called analysis (Morgenstern, 1976). However, it is clear that, while a large number of psychoanalysts remained rigid in their application of the analytic method, others were permitting themselves to adopt modifications of technique as appropriate.

As noted in Chapter 5, Eissler (1953) had recognised the need to make departures from 'standard' technique, and had introduced the notion of 'parameters', i.e., departures from the basic psychoanalytic method. But such parameters were intended to be used only when analysis would otherwise be impossible, and only if the analyst thought that they would be temporary expedients into which the patient would gain insight once 'standard' analysis had been resumed. The idea of parameters as temporary deviations from the 'standard' technique reinforced the idea that 'standard' technique was the only 'true' one, and for many analysts the need to use parameters was an uncomfortable sign of the failure of classical technique. However, the idea that classical technique could be deviated from, albeit temporarily, possibly played an unwitting part in licensing a degree of flexibility.

Looking back, Arnold Cooper has pointed out (1991) that throughout the 1960s and into the 1970s in the United States 'it was possible for most significant theoreticians to regard ego psychology as the touchstone for true psychoanalysis. Voices had been speaking for object-relations theory and later for self psychology, but there was a fairly tightly held definition of what was properly to be included within psychoanalysis' (p. 110). He then quotes what he calls Loewald's 'lament' (1970) in this connection.

> The new structural theory, based on the conceptions of narcissism, 'primary masochism', identification, introjection, and the formation of the superego, implied and expressed a new awareness of the fundamental importance of object ties for the formation of psychic structure. Although these ideas led further away from the old model, psychoanalysis nevertheless continued to cling to its theoretical premises. In many quarters there still seems to be a tendency to put up a 'no admittance' sign when metapsychological considerations point to object relations as being not merely regulative but essential constitutive factors in psychic structure formation.
>
> (1970 [1980], p. 299)

With the deaths of the members of the 'triumvirate' (Hartmann was the last to die, in 1970), the discrepancy between the official and the actual practice of psychoanalysis found expression in the United States in the development of new theoretical ideas which had profound implications for technique, and consequently for the conceptualisation of analytic aims. The most prominent of these ideas were those put forward by Heinz Kohut (especially in *The Analysis of the Self*, 1971). Kohut's ideas sent a shock wave through establishment psychoanalysis in the United States (they had little impact in Britain), causing positions to harden, but inevitably affecting the work of many analysts who did not, however, regard themselves as Kohutians, as belonging to the school of what came to be known as 'self psychology'.

Kohut summarised his view of a successful analysis as follows:

A successful analysis is one in which the analysand's formerly archaic needs for the responses of archaic selfobjects[1] are superseded by the experience of the availability of empathic resonance, the major constituent of the sense of security in adult life. Increased ability to verbalise, broadened insight, greater autonomy of ego functions, and increased control over impulsiveness may accompany these gains, but they are not the essence of cure. A treatment will be successful because . . . an analysand was able to reactivate, in a selfobject transference, the needs of a self that had been thwarted in childhood. In the analytic situation, these reactivated needs were kept alive and exposed, time and again, to the vicissitudes of optimal frustrations until the patient ultimately acquired the reliable ability to sustain his self with the aid of the selfobject resources available in his adult surroundings. According to self psychology, then, the essence of the psychoanalytic cure resides in a patient's newly acquired ability to identify and seek out appropriate selfobjects . . . as they present themselves in his realistic surroundings and to be sustained by them.

(1984, p. 77)

In addition to the importance of the selfobject concept, Kohut puts emphasis on the mechanism whereby the aim of analysis (which he sees as reorganization of the self) is achieved by the building of psychic structure through 'transmuting internalization', characterised by Moore and Fine (1990) as 'a process of effective internalization, initiated by the analyst's optimal nontraumatic frustration of the patient. It leads to structure formation whereby the self is able to execute vital selfobject functions in the absence of experiences with the selfobject. The process effects a translocation of the function from the person of the selfobject to the subject alone' (p. 176).

William Meissner (1991) describes this process somewhat differently.

The experience of the empathic bond with the analyst as selfobject allows the critical transmuting internalisations that build structure to take place . . . so that the experience of being understood (the empathic bond) becomes part of the psychic structure and the process of change. . . . The defect that was caused by parental deficiencies is cured by continuous interaction of the self with an empathic analytic selfobject who provides a new and corrective experience that corrects the defect.

(1991, pp. 56–57)

---

1 Kohut uses the term 'selfobject' in a very specific way. This has been described as follows (Moore and Fine, 1990): 'The selfobject is one's subjective experience of another person who provides a sustaining function to the self within a relationship, evoking and maintaining the self and the experience of selfhood by his or her presence or activity' (p. 178).

Kohut's views were not endorsed by Otto Kernberg, who had for a number of years been concerned with the same clinical problems, and had advocated a particular form of treatment of cases of borderline and narcissistic personality disorder. Kernberg 'sees narcissistic pathology as the result of the development of certain adaptive psychopathological *intra-psychic* structures rather than the outcome of early deficit, which Kohut sees as the result of a lack of development of normal narcissistic regulatory processes. For Kernberg, the group of narcissistic patients overlaps with the borderline group and consequently his approach to narcissistic disorders is the same as that taken by him in the treatment of borderline patients' (Sandler *et al.*, 1992, p. 77). Kernberg differs from Kohut in that he proposes that such cases be treated by a modified form of analysis, i.e., 'expressive' psychotherapy.[2] This approach involves the immediate analysis of primitive transferences as they arise in the here-and-now of the treatment. These transferences become modified into more mature forms as a result of their interpretation. Reconstruction of the past is avoided in the early stages of the therapy, and the therapist has to be extremely realistic and active. As Kernberg puts it,

> Transference analysis must focus both on the severity of acting out and on disturbances in the patient's external reality which may threaten the continuity of the treatment as well as the patient's psychosocial survival. Because of this and also because the treatment, as part of the acting out of primitive transferences, easily comes to replace life, transference interpretation must be codetermined by three sets of factors: (1) the conflicts predominating in immediate reality; (2) the overall specific goals of treatment, as well as the consistent differentiation of life goals from treatment goals (Ticho, 1972); and (3) what is immediately prevailing in the transference.
>
> (1984, p. 102)

For Kernberg the aims of treatment refer to

> developments and changes that occur as part of the psychotherapeutic relationship, and include the extent to which previously ego-syntonic pathological character traits may become ego dystonic, the extent to which capacities for self-awareness, introspection, and concern

---

2 One may well ask why this was not regarded as analysis. We may speculate that Kernberg referred to his technique as psychotherapy because these particular patients were seen three rather than four times a week. This caution was understandable in the prevailing conservative analytic climate in organised psychoanalysis in the United States.

develop under the influence of the treatment process, the extent to which patients are able to develop authentic object relationships with their therapists, and the extent to which patients' potential for negative therapeutic reaction can be resolved. . . . In order to achieve improvement in distorted ego functions, the patient must come to terms at some point with very real, serious limitations of what life has given him in his early years . . . and learn to accept the analyst realistically as a limited human being. . . . Coming to terms with severe defects in one's past requires the capacity to mourn and to work through such mourning; to accept aloneness; and to realistically accept that others may have what the patient himself may never be able to fully compensate for.

(1975, pp. 150, 174–175)

Both Kernberg and Kohut had begun putting forward new views on narcissistic pathology in the mid- and late 1960s, and indeed that decade saw the beginnings of many of the ideas which emerged so strongly in the 1970s. Although the majority of American psychoanalysts subscribed neither to Kohut's nor Kernberg's views, these ideas had a significant influence on the subsequent development of psychoanalysis.

Another influential figure on the American scene was Hans Loewald who, in writing on psychoanalytic theory and process in 1970, extended and elaborated the views he had expressed ten years previously in a paper on the therapeutic action of psychoanalysis. However, he now placed weight on the analyst–patient interaction as providing a 'psychic field' for the development of the patient. As analysts, whether we want to or not, we become, as Loewald put it, a weighty element and force in the psychic field. Loewald adds that, in significant periods of the analysis, we see externalisation of early internal relationships and conflicts, and this can lead, through the analytic work and appropriate insight and internalisation, to an alteration of the relatively archaic aspects of psychic organisation.

Loewald's paper reflects the turning of attention to the 'field' created by the interaction of both patient and analyst. This and the very specific focus on internal object relationships and their externalisation represented, together with the work of Kohut, a major factor in the change in orientation in psychoanalysis, and certainly contributed to the modifications of the traditional ego-psychological outlook which were to follow, not only in the United States but in other countries as well.[3]

The new emphasis on the interaction of patient and analyst in the analytic process was also evident in two related papers by Ernst Ticho (1971, 1972)

---

3 See Greenberg and Mitchell's interesting Object Relations in Psychoanalytic Theory (1983).

dealing explicitly with aims,[4] and which are worth presenting in some detail. Ticho (1971) points out that the treatment aim of the analyst ought to be identical with that of the analysand, to the extent that the analysand can gain a clear picture of the past and his future. Every diagnosis implies a prognosis, and every prognosis implies treatment aims. Ticho echoes Freud in saying that at the beginning of the treatment the diagnosis and prognosis is provisional and is corrected during the course of the treatment. The unconscious expectations of the patient are so closely tied to his neurosis that they can only become conscious through the patient's understanding of himself. In this Ticho differentiates between the conscious and unconscious aims of the patient. He points out that among analysts there is now greater interest in the study of the healthy personality, and suggests that we need to describe mental health in a dynamic rather than in a static way; the healthy personality grows, while the neurotic one remains at a standstill. Ticho's view has consistently been that progress in the analysis can be described in the dynamic sense of *moving towards* mental health, rather than in terms of having achieved a *state* of mental health.

In 1972 Ticho continues the themes he developed in his earlier paper and says

> Mental illness may be looked upon as an interruption and distortion of developmental processes. Psychoanalysis is a treatment method that aims at the removal of the causes of such an interruption so that development can be resumed. If this treatment goal is achieved it makes it possible for the patient to reach his life goals. A clinical distinction between treatment goals and life goals is important for the conduct of therapy, and this can be done despite their partial overlap. *Life goals* are the goals the patient would seek to attain if he could put his potentialities to use. In other words, they are the goals the patient would aim at if his 'true self' (Winnicott, 1960b) and his creativity were freed. *Treatment goals* concern [the analytic] removal of obstacles to the patient's discovery of what his potentialities are.
>
> (1972, p. 315)

Ticho goes on to say that changes in the initial life goals will occur during the course of the analysis as the patient becomes aware of the unconscious goals closely connected with his neurosis, and comments:

> When the patient understands his neurosis he will be in a position to assess the contradiction between conscious and unconscious goals; only then can he arrive at unified treatment goals. At this point he

---

4 The first of these papers was published in German and not translated.

88

will have a better understanding of his potentialities and will begin to define his life goals in a more rational way.

(1972, pp. 315–316)

Ticho's reference to the patient's better understanding of his potentialities as a result (and therefore aim) of analysis clarifies the ambiguity inherent in his reference to analysis removing the causes for interruption of the patient's development so that development can be resumed. Our own view in this connection is that a *distorted* development, once critical childhood developmental phases have been passed, can never be corrected in the sense of 'starting again', of restarting blocked 'normal' development. Rather, the patient may be able to develop compensatory or rectifying psychic structures which reflect different solutions to internal conflict and which enable him to be psychologically 'healthier'.

Ticho then divides life goals into *professional* and *personal* goals. Professional life goals refer to achievements in one's chosen work. Personal life goals refer to what kind of human being one would like to be. Both goals are dependent on conscious and unconscious ideals (we would add that life goals and treatment goals are mutually interdependent), and may not be fully achieved by the end of the analysis. Rather, they may only come to fruition in the postanalytic phase, but even then they will be limited by irreversible aspects of the patient's developmental history.

Among the list of indications that a termination phase has been reached are the following, which are of interest in their relation to analytic aims. The criteria given by Ticho include the assessment of the quality of the relationship (the 'real relationship') between analyst and patient, and whether the relationship moves in the direction of becoming one between equals that will enable the patient to establish equally mature relationships with other people in his life. Further criteria are: does the patient perceive the analyst in realistic terms? Have the patient's separation anxieties and his approach to the 'new beginning' been analysed? What are the transference residues? And what is the patient's future growth potential, his ability to define life goals, and to follow them creatively? In these criteria we can see a move from classical ego psychology to a heightened concern with object relationships, and with the way in which these manifest themselves in the analysis.

Hal Hurn (1971) can be regarded as supplementing Ticho's view in a discussion of indications that the patient has entered the terminal phase of analysis. He regards this phase as beginning with signs that the patient has significantly accepted the impossibility of obtaining infantile gratification from the analyst. At the same time, the analyst is increasingly experienced as a contemporary real object, defined predominantly by his real function for the patient, and his meaning as a figure with whom the infantile neurosis had been resolved. All of this results in the patient becoming more comfortable in the analytic work and in a significant augmentation of the therapeutic alliance. However, the analyst in turn perceives a corresponding change in his own ways of responding to the patient. He senses a reduced transference pressure, including the pressure to function as whatever transference figure the patient had yearned for. The analyst then feels a certain increase in comfort, as he does not need to be so much on the alert for untoward transferences from his patient. The separation between patient and analyst is a separation between two adults whose relationship has been in the nature of collaborative work. Reactions emotionally appropriate to each are expectable and have either a mourning-like character or one that portends mourning. There should be a visible shifting of emotional interests to extra-analytic concerns. Finally, in Hurn's view, the tendency to perceive the analyst objectively and without transference distortion should be regarded as approaching but never quite reaching the actuality of the analyst 'asymptotically'. Hurn's criteria for termination focus on the intra-analytic changes that analysis can bring about. Enduring intrapsychic modifications linked with some concept of mental health are not spelled out among the criteria. Clearly Hurn's criteria involve an underlying assumption that successful negotiation of the terminal phase results in persisting internal changes in the patient. The mood of the 1970s is reflected in the emphasis placed by such authors as Hurn and Ticho on the changes in both partners in the analytic couple.

During the 1970s we can also see the beginnings of a re-emphasis on superego change as a criterion for termination of analysis and consequently also as an analytic aim. The desirability of lessening the harshness of the superego through analysis had been a prominent feature of the work of the early Freudians (Chapter 2). The newer concern with object relationships revived the earlier tendency to view the relationship of ego to superego, as seen in the analysis, not only in terms of structural conflict but in terms of internal object relations as well. This is reflected in a panel discussion of the American Psychoanalytic Association on 'Termination: problems and techniques' (reported by Robbins, 1975), where Greenson comments that 'it is beneficial for a patient to identify with the analyst's helpful qualities, i.e., that his identifications and superego changes [brought about by analysis] do not go to form a harsh, critical, or indulgent superego, but that the patient takes into himself qualities of self-help which once were externalised in the analyst' (Robbins, 1975, p. 173).

It is striking that by the mid-1970s the grip of the ego-psychological viewpoint on psychoanalysis in the United States continued to diminish. This was in part a consequence of interest in the ideas put forward by the self psychologists and the object-relations theorists – for example, Winnicott and Fairbairn in Britain and such authors as Margaret Mahler and Arnold Modell in the US. It was also a result of emerging concerns about psychoanalytic theory and technique, concerns which had been growing beneath the surface in the preceding years. So we see a stimulus to re-evaluate psychoanalytic theory, in particular in its application to practice. The mid-1970s saw a panel of the American Psychoanalytic Association on 'Current concepts of the psychoanalytic process' (reported by Morgenstern, 1976). The panel included an exploration of the contribution of child observation studies to the understanding of the psychoanalytic process. The further evolution and acknowledgement of a developmental perspective in psychoanalytic theory and technique was strongly influenced by the significant contributions of Margaret Mahler (Mahler *et al.*, 1975). A number of authors (for example, see Erikson, 1950; Spitz, 1957, 1965; Winnicott, 1960a, 1960b, 1962; A. Freud, 1963, 1965; Klein, 1975) had, on the basis of their work with children, applied new developmental insights to the understanding of the adult. Mahler and her colleagues were able, however, extrapolating from their work with psychotic children, to propose a powerful new framework for normal development which emphasised early processes of separation–individuation, and which could be placed alongside Freud's schema of psychosexual development. In short, the view was taken in the panel discussion that analysis must include among its aims the rectification in the adult of processes and capacities which may have been hindered during the course of normal development – for example, the developing child's capacity for separation–individuation.

It is interesting that the panel had originally been charged with discussing current concepts of the therapeutic process, but the participants had expressed the wish to change the word 'therapeutic' to 'psychoanalytic' in the title of the panel. In this connection Morgenstern points out that

> inasmuch as we have increasingly seen our analytic role less as treaters of illness and more as understanders of mental processes, we are less concerned with what one properly could call a therapeutic process and more with what we describe as a psychoanalytic process. Thus less encumbered with therapeutic zeal, we have enabled ourselves to become more effective as analysts of a wider scope of our patient's psychological life.
>
> (1976, p. 194)

We can see reflected here a further turning away from the view of analysis as a therapeutic tool, almost certainly because of the number of competing 'psychological' therapies which aimed at curing the patient of his illness. It was necessary for psychoanalysis to establish its identity clearly, and to differentiate itself from the other therapies. The way to do this was to retreat from the therapeutic stance and to re-emphasise the aim of self-understanding through self-exploration. Anxiety had certainly been aroused among analysts by the slow growth and lessened influence of organised psychoanalysis in comparison with the exponential growth of other therapies, including psychoanalytically based psychotherapies and pharmacotherapy. This phenomenon can be seen as a reflection of the fact that, in those countries where the mushrooming of other therapies has occurred, there has been a socio-economically determined pressure towards pragmatism and rapid cures. It is worth recalling that Eissler, in remarking on the aims of psychoanalysis and of psychotherapy, had said a decade earlier (1963) that

> it must be acknowledged that there are patients who cannot do better than to adjust or to be successful, whose self is not strong enough to bear truth. The analyst must never become an evangelist: insight into psychological processes, to the analyst an end in itself, is usually aspired to by patients for purely therapeutic reasons. It is one of the many apparent paradoxes I have encountered in the science of man's mind that just those patients who are less interested in their therapy, but become absorbed in the delight of increasing their knowledge of self have, in my experience, a better chance of recovering from their psychopathology than those who adhere to what psychoanalysis offers at the social level – a therapy.
>
> (1963, pp. 461–462)

Even earlier, the tendency to move from a therapeutic stance had been evident when, for example, Karl Menninger attempted to characterise the uniqueness of psychoanalysis by emphasising how much more it involved than symptom cure.

> In the early days psychoanalysis was very much under the influence of the point of view according to which a disappearance of symptoms indicates a recession of the illness. But today we no longer regard this as an adequate criterion. The patient who has fully recovered from an illness with the aid of psychoanalysis will not have become his old self again; rather he has become (we trust) an enlarged, an improved, indeed a *new* self.
>
> (1958, p. 156)

The renewed tendency to diminish the importance of the therapeutic aspect of psychoanalysis was to gain strength in the 1970s. In the context of a discussion of psychotherapy and psychoanalysis, at a Pre-Congress Meeting on Training held in New York in 1979 by the International Psychoanalytical Association, Leo Stone endorsed the view that psychoanalysis was more than a treatment method:

> We can accept the classical psychoanalytic situation as it is broadly and usually understood, regardless of certain nuances of difference in

92

point of view. For the broad outlines and goals remain essentially the same, in comparison with the various forms of psychotherapy. The (manifestly) nonpurposive, nonselective emphasis on breadth and spontaneity of communication, with the built-in deprivations of the process, is calculated to produce a sweeping exposure of the personality and, by the same token, a sweeping and deep transference regression, culminating in a broad, multifaceted transference neurosis. . . . Therapeutic effect is, so to speak, a 'byproduct', a result of spontaneous adaptive thrust.

(1982, p. 83)

Such reduction of emphasis on symptomatic improvement has a parallel in the lessened emphasis put by such authors as Fritz Morgenthaler (1978) on social adaptation. Morgenthaler is quite emphatic in saying that analysis is not intended to fit the patient to society, to make him a good student and conforming social person. In his view the analytic process follows the transference and has lines of development which do not correspond to the structures of the society in which we live. The analytic process is not a means of attaining the end of getting happier and happier in a linear fashion; nor is the fulfilment of such expectations a criterion for terminating an analysis.

The complex situation in the mid-1970s, when psychoanalysis was developing in several different directions, was clearly brought out in 1975, when the International Psychoanalytical Association's Congress in London held a panel on 'The changing expectations of patients and psychoanalysts today' (reported by Cramer and Flournoy, 1976). The outcome of this illuminating panel, in which Wolfgang Loch, Jacob Arlow, Otto Kernberg, Joyce McDougall and Kjell Øhrberg participated, is summed up by the reporters who emphasise the expectations patients now have of analysts and stress that this expectation is both interpersonal and intrapsychic in nature; it is intimately linked to the analytic situation and process:

Seen from without, reciprocal expectations might have changed according to historical developments in psychoanalytic theory: one could observe a change from expecting symptom resolution to hoping for a better integrating function of the ego, according to ego psychology formulations. From the expectations of making unconscious infantile conflicts conscious, one may hope to repair the object, primarily the mother, according to Kleinian theory. One may thus describe many changing expectations according to changes in *theory*.

Seen from within, changing expectations could be formulated at different levels. One may, for example, attempt to elicit changing expectations during the unfolding of the analysis. This was not the topic of the meeting; yet with the lengthening of cures [analyses], the analyst is open to evolution and changes in psychoanalytic theory. This must affect his expectations at different stages of the analysis, just as the natural unfolding of the analysis will also alter the expectations of both patient and analyst.

It seemed that during this Congress the problem of reciprocal expectations was often dealt with . . . in new ways: analysts and patients would no longer expect to resolve specific problems, to uncover hidden meaning, to refind affects that seemed erased; they would seek more to 'get along together'. This might reflect present-day vicissitudes of man; man seeks to escape from his narcissistic loneliness which confronts him more with the problem of an absence of objects rather than with one absent object. In this conjunction, it may be that the analysand perceives dimly that just as getting along together is really impossible, it is an impossible task to wish for the complete removal of his suffering – as was suggested by some discussants – just as it might be Utopian to wish for the persistence of his suffering according to his masochistic leanings. Hence, what might be more important, according to some, is the creation of a 'playing space', an analytic field where the analysand will be able to symbolize his basic wishes within the framework provided by the analyst and without fear of a catastrophe. In this type of analytic field, the analyst will be not only a witness, but also a participant in this creative play; he may remain silent, sometimes passive, sometimes active, but he will always be there. The reciprocal expectations then take place within the context of a dedramatized relationship, with less demanding expectations regarding an ideal result of the type 'where id was, there ego shall be'.

(1976, pp. 426–427)

In their report on this panel Cramer and Flournoy make a telling point when they emphasise the degree to which the current theory of the psychoanalyst influences both the analyst's and the patient's expectations of what analysis can achieve.

At the same congress another panel relevant to the topic of aims was held. This was a discussion on 'The fundamentals of psychic change in clinic practice' (reported by Naiman, 1976) in which increased emphasis appeared to be placed on the need to bring about fundamental changes in internal object relationships. Betty Joseph, expressing a Kleinian view, saw such changes as involving the diminution of processes of splitting and projection into objects, which result in distortions in object relationships. As a consequence 'more benign and realistic objects can be introduced into the ego and superego' (quoted by Naiman, p. 413). In this connection Sandler commented that psychic changes normally occur throughout life, and there are similarities between those which occur outside and inside analysis. As life progresses we form new 'solutions' to the problems imposed on us. The old solutions do not disappear, but remain latent or may be integrated into newer solutions. In analysis we do not 'undo' past modes of functioning – rather, we help the patient's ego to form new solutions which may give the patient a greater degree of autonomy, lessen his discomfort and, one hopes, make him happier. If there is symptom change, however, the structures behind the symptoms are not lost, but rather their use is suspended. From this point of view, in which the superego introjects are considered as mental 'structures', it is not the objects constituting the patient's superego which change, but rather the ego's relation to the existing superego introjects (although clearly further introjection could take place). With greater autonomy one does not pay as much attention to these introjects, just as one normally becomes less dependent on one's parents during development. (Elizabeth Spillius [personal communication] points out that, rather than to think in terms of 'repairing' the object, it might be more appropriate, in the Kleinian view, to expect changes in the *attitude* towards the relationship with the object.) Looking back, we would say that lessening of splitting and projection described by Joseph would be a major contribution to the formation of new 'solutions' which function to allow the patient to accept back into his self-representation aspects of his self which had been rendered un-acceptable in the course of the development of his internal object relationships.

The position taken by Sandler carries the implication that states of stress (of internal or external origin) may, even in the most well-analysed patient, bring about regression to heightened dependency on the internal superego objects. The same tendency would show itself in regard to symptoms in general. It would follow that one of the aims of psychoanalysis would be to increase the patient's capacity to tolerate temporary regression and to recover from it.

To conclude . . .

Throughout the 1970s less is said than in the previous decades about conflict between psychic structures, although a substantial hard core of 'classical' ego- psychological formulations in regard to analytic aims persists to this day. We can see a growing preoccupation with aims in terms of changes in the patient's 'self' and in the internal relations between self and object brought about through the analysis. The patient's and the analyst's analytic goals are compared and contrasted, and the gaining and elaboration of the selfanalytic function (which had been discussed on and off in the past, e.g. by Gertrude Ticho, 1967) is given more prominence. Although not always explicit, we can see in the writings of North American psycho-analysts the influence of British views, particularly of such writers as Melanie Klein and Donald Winnicott in their emphasis on internal object relationships and on the influence on development of early infantile experiences (although these writers and their followers had been influential in Europe and Latin America for some considerable time). What was marked in the 1970s was the intensity of the disputes between the proponents of different theories. As we shall see, this situation was to change with the acceptance of the coexistence of different viewpoints and their mutual influence.

8

Pragmatism and integration in contemporary psychoanalysis

As different theoretical perspectives developed in psychoanalysis, questions regarding aims were formulated by protagonists of different schools in terms of their own particular theoretical orientations. Nevertheless, as might be expected, there were conservative writers who reiterated their theoretical positions without taking into account changes which had occurred as a consequence of the cross-fertilisation of ideas. It is true that throughout the development of psychoanalysis the persistence of past formulations into the present has had a certain stabilising function, and has prevented basic psychoanalytic ideas being jettisoned too readily. But it is equally true that the conservatism resulting from the influence of previous generations of psychoanalysts, because of the specific nature of psycho-analytic education, has slowed down productive development in the field when compared with other scientific disciplines. However, during the 1980s a growing process of dialogue and confrontation between the proponents of different analytical viewpoints became evident. Views other than one's own had to be understood and considered in order to debate them; more importance was attached to the presentation and discussion of clinical material by analysts who had different orientations; and as a consequence there was an increasing capacity to view other people's theories and one's own as theories rather than as fixed systems of belief.

The theme of an International Psychoanalytical Congress in New York in 1979 was 'Clinical issues in psychoanalysis', and the focus on clinical processes at that congress adumbrated some of the developments in the years that followed. In his concluding remarks to the congress, Sidney Furst (1980) summed up the situation as he saw it then: 'Clinical issues occupy a special position in our field. On the one hand they are first order derivatives of the observations which we make in our daily work; on the other they constitute the immediate base for theory formation. Thus, their intermediate position between observation and theory permits them to serve as a bridge, linking the two. This linkage, and its corollary, the linkage between understanding and cure, are the hallmarks of psycho-analysis, which distinguish it from all other forms of treatment for mental disorder' (p. 225). With regard to the aims of psychoanalysis, discussed in a panel at the congress on 'The closing phase of the psychoanalytic treatment of adults and the goals of psychoanalysis', Furst points out that over the years ego psychologists have placed emphasis on criteria expressed in terms of structural change (i.e., improvement in reality testing, the achievement of higher levels of psychic functioning and adaptive behavioural change); yet in practice there is now less expectation that such goals can be fully attained.

Furst drew attention to common elements in the various psychoanalytic theoretical perspectives current at the time.

> The newer psychoanalytic schools of thought subscribe in varying degree to goals of the classical school, the improvement of reality testing and acquisition of insight being two examples. However, to the extent that the analytic process includes penetration of deepest levels of pre-verbal experience, sometimes referred to as the psychotic core, they are expressed in terms of propositions regarding pathogenesis rather than clinical criteria. Other goals such as the 'restoration of the cohesive self', or 'to be what one is', may be regarded as variants of, or implicit in the classical model, though the techniques employed in achieving them differ. Criteria for termin-ation according to the new models are usually conceived more in terms of the patient's ability to relinquish the active, affective encounter with the analyst, usually by introjecting him, and to complete the work of mourning for lost objects and parts of the self.
>
> (1980, p. 233)

These comments emphasise underlying similarities between different psychoanalytic viewpoints. But striking differences in formulation were evident in the panel. For example, Herbert Gaskill (1980) put forward the classical view, reiterating the conceptualisations of American ego psychologists in previous decades. However, Leon Grinberg, who was strongly influenced by the work of Melanie Klein and Wilfred Bion, expressed his concerns about the analyst having 'aims' in his work with his patient:

> We 'saturate' the development of the psychoanalytic relationship with the aprioristic idea of 'leading' our patients to achieve the therapeutic goals we have already fixed for them from the very beginning . . . when considering these criteria, the accent has been almost exclusively put on the personality of the analysand . . . it is important to take into account also that which concerns the

personality of the analyst with his neurotic and/or psychotic remnant
. . . which can disturb his creative work.

(1980, pp. 34–35)

While the gaining of insight can be considered to be fundamental to all
psychoanalytic approaches, Grinberg considers the question from the
specific point of view of the 'love of truth'.[1]

> The concept of insight is related to that knowledge which stems from
> the experiences of deep change and mental growth helping the
> patient to get near to 'being his own truth', with the need to accept
> the corresponding responsibility. It is important to differentiate this
> authentic insight, so close to the getting near to the truth, from all
> other types of intellectual knowledge or 'pseudo-insight' which tends
> towards the opposite, that is, the avoidance of the truth.

(1980, p. 35)

We want to stress here that different formulations of the sort expressed
by Gaskill and Grinberg existed side by side at the turn of the decade. In
relation to this Horacio Etchegoyen's comment that 'the criteria for a cure
will be different depending on the theoretical supports from which we
attempt to approach them' is of interest. He says

> Hartmann's psychology of adaptation, for example, leads to the idea
> that the termination of analysis implies reinforcing the area free of
> conflict and a sufficiently adaptive ego functioning, whereas the
> Kleinian school will emphasise working through the depressive
> anxieties. Lacan will say, acidly undervaluing the psychology of
> adaptation, that a good ending sanctions the subject's submission to
> the symbolic order, and Winnicott will maintain that the analysand
> will have acquired his true self and in accepting disillusionment
> sufficiently will now know how much he owes his mother.

(1991a, pp. 617–618)

Meissner (1991) describes the situation succinctly:

> Different approaches seem to focus on different therapeutic out-
> comes. Ego psychologists emphasise the alteration of psychic
> structure on the basis of conflict resolution and internalisation; self

---

[1] Grinberg here makes use of a notion of 'truth' which is derived from Bion (1970).
Although Grinberg qualifies the notion by referring to 'the patient's own truth', many
analysts would have reservations about the use of the concept of 'truth' in this
context. Nevertheless, few would quarrel with Grinberg's statement that 'it is not
enough that a patient knows that he has envy, but rather that he should feel that he *is*
envious and should be able to tolerate it' (1980, p. 30).

psychologists also emphasise changes in structure, but see it more in terms of transmuting internalisations resulting in renewed psychic growth; hermeneuticists focus on the more comprehensive and coherent narrative of the self; the object relations view stresses the modifications of the inner representational world and the correspondingly more adaptive relations with external objects; and the information processing approach envisions change of false belief systems and other cognitive apprehensions.

(1991, p. 49)

But during the 1980s there was a growing recognition of the relativity, and at the same time of a degree of underlying similarity, of different approaches. This culminated in such papers as Robert Wallerstein's 'One psychoanalysis or many?' (1988). He points out there that it is actually the *clinical* situation which is the 'common ground'.

In spite of these theoretical differences, which certainly exist, Etchegoyen's final remark is to the point, when he says that 'while the subject of curative factors leads us inexorably to the most complicated theoretical problems of our discipline and to the point of possibly a major confrontation of the schools, it is also true that in the practice of the consulting room there is a broad enough agreement, which is surprising, as to the evaluation of the analysand's progress' (1991a, p. 623).

These issues had, only a short while earlier, found expression in the theme of the International Congress in Rome in 1989 (chosen by Wallerstein, who was then President of the International Association), i.e., 'Common ground in psychoanalysis: clinical aims and process'.[2] In the succeeding years, however, the 'common ground' position has been criticised as too sweeping (see, for example, the panel discussion on 'Effects of theory on psychoanalytic technique and on the development of psychoanalytic process', reported by E. Schuker, 1990). While a degree of common ground is generally acknowledged, nevertheless differences in psychoanalytic technique are more and more to be seen as powerful determinants of the outcome of an analysis. Awareness of this has fostered a

---

2 A comment by Milton Viederman gives an interesting perspective on the issue of 'common ground'. He says that 'change occurs not only by analysis of the transference or by analysis of conflict as it relates to experiences in the outside world, but also in the context of transactions between analyst and patient as they pertain to dialogue with the patient's life. That successful outcomes in analysis may occur with analysts of widely differing theoretical persuasions can be understood as related to the internalisation of the dialogue between analyst and patient which, though guided by a theoretical model, is powerfully influenced by the special quality of their relationship (1991, pp. 486–487).

noticeable interaction, with consequent mutual influence of the different 'schools' on one another. At the same time there has been a more general realisation that the adequacy of a theoretical position can only be assessed by the evaluation of clinical material. So we get the increased use of illustrative vignettes in discussions of one or other specific aspect of the clinical process. Arnold Cooper put it, somewhat ironically, in a useful review of concepts of change and therapeutic effectiveness.[3]

> In our current climate of theoretical pluralism, there has been a shift in approach, and analysts are meticulously trying to describe what occurs during a session, or even a moment of analytic work . . . there is, however, a tendency for analysts to believe that if they describe what occurred during a session, they have described the source of therapeutic action.
>
> (1989, p. 6)

Linked with the attention being paid to the details of the clinical process was a tendency during the 1980s and 1990s to displace the issue of aims on to a concern with issues of *psychic change*, and with the problem of the factors which bring about or facilitate such change. For example we find that there are numerous contemporary contributions on the topic of psychic change from different theoretical and clinical analytic perspectives (see especially Horowitz *et al.*, 1993). Whereas the concern with processes of psychic change has been present to varying degree throughout the history of psychoanalysis, it has become particularly marked because of the progressively sophisticated discussion of the differences between the various psychoanalytic approaches. The preoccupation with processes of psychic change has led to a diminution of attention to outcome aims formulated in terms of states of mental health (freedom from symptoms, happiness, capacity for work and love, etc.), a topic which had engaged psychoanalysts much more in the past. The emphasis on psychic change and on issues of technique is probably in part a result of the pressure on analysts, forced upon them by differences in analytic approach, to examine what it is that actually goes on between analyst and patient. With this, attention has been focused on theoretical concepts as *useful constructs* for the

---

3 Michael Bader, in a paper on 'The tendency to neglect therapeutic aims in psychoanalysis', speaks of the 'tendency to turn away from a rigorous attempt to keep therapeutic outcome in our analytic cross-hairs and, instead, to focus more and more on those small units of intra-analytic behaviour that can be studied' (1994, p. 248). Bader also comments that 'analysts want to cure their patients but tend to regard this therapeutic ambition as a potential obstacle in their work' (p. 247). Bader's paper is valuable as it shows clearly how analysts may defend against their wish to cure by emphasising process goals. Such an emphasis also avoids the difficulties inherent in defining outcome criteria.

analytic work rather than as absolutes. So, for example, the concept of the transference neurosis has been challenged, and for many analysts is regarded as at best one variety of transference.[4] Cooper's paper on the topic (1987) is entitled 'The transference neurosis: a concept ready for retirement', and we would concur with this.

A result of the critical evaluation of the concept is that a longstanding 'officially' stated aim of psychoanalysis, namely the aim of resolving the patient's transference *neurosis*, has to be questioned. However, the aim of resolving as far as possible the patient's transference (including the external-isations of internal object relationships) would seem to be an appropriate objective of the analytic work as it is brought to an end.

Alongside the preoccupation with processes of psychic change has been a greater concern with *intermediate* aims during the course of treatment. This seems to be true of the various different approaches, and is well exemplified by Rangell's ego-psychological description of a sequence of steps in therapy (1987). He describes in detail a progression in terms of changes aimed for in the patient.[5] Such a formally stated sequence of aimed-for changes can be regarded as reflecting a conservative technical approach in the United States, in which, as Cooper (1989, p. 12) points out, 'the role of the analyst is as a benign interpreter of reality, who, through his interpretations, is internalised as a temporary new object, helping to make the unconscious conscious, and modifying the superego. Classical analytic neutrality is preserved, and the emphasis is on the change in psychic structures.'

Whereas Rangell's formulations do not reflect the influence of other

---

4 See the interesting panel discussion on 'Concepts and controversies about the transference neurosis', reported by Shaw (1991).
5 Rangell summarises the progressive steps in the analytic process as follows: (1) the store of conscious memories is enlarged; (2) the traumatic aspects of repressed memories are admitted into consciousness and are contained by the observing and assessing ego of the patient; (3) the traumatic contents are exposed, understood, abreacted, mastered and worked through. Their compelling power is diminished and the ego becomes freer; (4) consequent on the diminution of traumatic aspects of the past, the ego, in trial actions, experiences signals of anxiety less often; (5) fewer defences are now needed and safety signals occur more often. The changes lead to a new freedom of the ego which 'develops an increased capacity to tolerate anxiety and frustration. This reveals itself in its new handling of the intrapsychic process' (p. 242); (6) ego autonomy is expanded and the ego freed for widened choice; (7) all psychic structures come in for improved and adaptive changes. Thus 'the superego is modified to an internal composition more attuned to ego- and culture-syntony' (p. 242); (8) the id also changes; (9) the result of these changes is an improved self-representation within the ego. The ego has an increased 'relative autonomy'; (10) secondary gains have to be surrendered by means of further 'working through'.

schools, Kohut's views as expressed in his last book, *How Does Analysis Cure?* (1984), do show a subtle shift of emphasis in the direction of accommodating elements from other approaches, while retaining the distinct features of self psychology. Similarly, Arnold Goldberg, in speaking of the development of a shared meaning between patient and analyst (1987), reflects the tendency beginning in the 1980s for cross-fertilisation between different orientations in elaborating the object-relational aspect of Kohutian theory. The same tendency is shown in Kohut (1984) who, while re-emphasising the point that the aim of psychoanalysis is the rebuilding of the structure *of the self* (rather than the ego or superego), says that

> whereas self psychology relies on the same tools as traditional analysis (interpretation followed by working through in an atmosphere of abstinence) to bring about the analytic cure, self psychology sees in a different light not only the results that are achieved, but also the very role that interpretation and working through play in the analytic process.
>
> (1984, p. 75)

He sees the curative process in analysis as

> a three-step movement, the first two steps of which may be described as defence analysis and the unfolding of the transferences, while the third step – the essential one because it defines the aim and the result of the cure – is the opening of a path of empathy between self and selfobject, specifically, the establishment of empathic in-tuneness between self and selfobject on mature adult levels. This new channel of empathy permanently takes the place of the formerly repressed or split-off archaic narcissistic relationship; it supplants the bondage that had formerly tied the archaic self to the archaic selfobject.
>
> (1984, pp. 65–66)

Cooper (1989) comments on this in the following way:

> While self psychologists have stressed the empathic failure of the primary caretaker as the major aetiologic factor in psychopathologic development, and some have indicated that the analyst's empathy is itself the curative 'replacement' therapy, that is not Kohut's view in his final work. The empathic bond of analyst and patient is a precondition for psychoanalytic work . . . [which] however still consists of interpretation in the transference. . . . Again, with shifts in emphasis, and with a different theoretical role for the self as a motivating force, Kohut can be seen as placing himself within the mainstream of the newer object-relational and developmental ideas of the mode of therapeutic action.
>
> (1989, p. 18)

It is worth noting that although there is a tendency to speak of object-relational theorists (as Cooper does) as if they represented a coherent 'school', this is not in fact the case. Under the heading 'object-relational' are grouped those whose ideas have developed from, for example, the theories of such different British psychoanalysts as Ronald Fairbairn, Michael Balint, Donald Winnicott and members of the Kleinian school. In the United States there have been such theorists as Edith Jacobson (1954, 1964), Hans Loewald (1960, 1970), Otto Kernberg (1975) and Arnold Modell (1976). Relevant, too, are more recent discussions (e.g. Greenberg and Mitchell, 1983; Greenberg, 1991; Mitchell, 1988). Nevertheless, in spite of the various differences between object-relational theorists (in, for example, differences in regard to the influence of the real external environment) there is a degree of common ground. There is an emphasis in the analytic therapy on the interaction between patient and analyst, and an emphasis in the aim of analysis on changes in the patient's relation to his self and to his objects, both external and internal.

While Kleinian psychoanalysts are much concerned with the development of internal object relationships, particularly as created and modified by unconscious phantasy, they cannot be regarded as 'pure' object-relations theorists because of the emphasis they place on the role of the drives, in particular the death instinct (for a comprehensive account of Kleinian theory and practice, see Spillius, 1988a, 1988b). Melanie Klein's view of the aim of psychoanalysis, as described earlier (Chapter 4), was inferred from her paper on termination (1950). The aim was seen as the lessening of persecutory and depressive anxieties and dealing satisfactorily with the resultant situation of mourning. More recently, in a paper on 'The aim of psychoanalysis' (1989), John Steiner has elaborated the Kleinian view from the standpoint of the central aim of 'the understanding and alleviation of mental illness and suffering and the promotion of growth and development in the individual patient'. Steiner takes the view that Melanie Klein's discovery of schizoid mechanisms, in particular projective identification (1946), fundamentally alters the aims of psychoanalysis. He describes Klein's view of projective identification as a process in which

> a primitive mechanism in which part of the self is split off and projected into the object. The aim is sometimes to get rid of unwanted attributes and sometimes to attack and control the object, but sometimes it also serves as a primitive means of communication with the object. An important consequence of this mechanism is that a lack of separateness between self and object results and it becomes unclear which attributes belong to self and which belong to the object. . . .
> The aim of psychoanalysis according to this model is to help the

104

patient find an integration and reacquire parts of herself which were previously lost through projective identification.[6]

(1989, pp. 112–113, 115)

It is worth noting that here we can see a return, within Kleinian thinking, to the use of the notion of resistance as something other than an attempt to destroy the analyst or the analytic work. This is almost certainly a consequence of the interaction over many years of members of the different groups within the British Psychoanalytical Society.

Steiner points out that, after a period of therapeutic optimism and confidence, during which it seemed possible to treat even very disturbed patients by Melanie Klein's approach, it became clear that 'it was often not easy for the patient to face the psychic reality which emerged if he began to take back into himself previously split-off parts' (p. 115). Frequently the acceptance back into the self of the destructive forces in the personality mobilised intense resistances to the analytic work. Projective identification obscures the distinction between self and object, and what is necessary to achieve the aim of psychoanalysis, says Steiner, is for a process of mourning to be worked through so that the object

> is perceived more realistically and the self is enriched, but as a consequence the individual is more clearly aware of a separateness of self and object, and recognises more clearly what belongs to the self and what belongs to the object. Separateness makes one aware of both good and bad aspects of the object and the denial of separateness consequently serves as a protection against both frustration and envy. . . . If reality cannot be faced mourning cannot proceed and the patient cannot regain the parts of the self he has disowned. . . . If this reality is worked through, a quantum of mourning takes place as the object is relinquished and a quantum of self is withdrawn from the object and returned to the ego ['ego' in this context is probably better read as 'self']. The ego is thereby strengthened and the object is in a measure seen more realistically. This then means that conflict is tackled with greater resources and there is a lessening of the need to evade reality.

(1989, pp. 116–117, 119)

In summary, then, the aim of psychoanalysis in this view is to help the patient take back projected parts of the self and to reintegrate them into the personality.

The Kleinian perspective has been absorbed to varying degrees into the work of contemporary mainstream psychoanalysts. For example Joseph and

---

6 See Sandler (1987) for a full discussion of the projective identification concept.

Anne-Marie Sandler, members of the Contemporary Freudian Group in the British Society, state the aim of analysis in a way which shows the influence of Kleinian propositions. Whereas Kleinian theory holds that the aim of analysis is to enable the patient to restore to the self the split-off parts which have been dealt with by projective identification (see also Hinshelwood, 1989), Sandler and Sandler have proposed the following formulation (1983):

> The analyst aims to help the patient eventually to accept the infantile wishful aspects of himself which have aroused painful conflict and have become threatening during the course of his development. As a consequence he strives to get the patient to tolerate the . . . *derivatives* of these parts of himself in his conscious thinking and phantasies. To put it another way: a major analytic goal is to get the patient to become friends with the previously unacceptable parts of himself, to get on good terms with previously threatening wishes and phantasies. To do this means that the analyst has to provide, through his interpretations and the way he gives them, an atmosphere of tolerance of the infantile, the perverse and the ridiculous, an atmosphere which the patient can make part of his own attitudes towards himself, which he can internalise along with the understanding he has reached in his joint work with the analyst.[7]
>
> (1983, p. 423)

The analytic aim of enabling split-off and rejected parts of the self to be brought back into the self is also implied in an earlier remark by Loewald (1981) to the effect that experiences regressively revived in the analysis can have a very positive aspect in that, as he put it, 'in analysis they are given a chance to return from the repressed Unconscious – not only in order to find more advanced expression and integration in a developmental sense, but for their own sake; through them we regain access to the fresh immediacy and intensity of living' (p. 29).

A statement by Jacob Arlow (1987) expresses a similar viewpoint:

> Treatment, then, becomes a matter, not of recollecting and purging one's self of a noxious memory from the past; it becomes instead a matter of knowing and mastering a persistently disturbing influence in the present. . . . The interaction between the analyst's interventions and the patient's response exposes the nature of the compromise formations. This process deepens the patient's understanding of how his mind works and facilitates achieving insight. Thera-

---

[7] The Sandlers consider that a whole variety of defences, including (but not subsumed under the heading of) projective identification, are involved in the process of splitting off aspects of the self-representation.

peutically, this may lead to a realignment of the forces in conflict, eventuating in more adaptive, less conflictual compromise formations. As Brenner (1976) has pointed out, conflicts do not disappear as a result of treatment, but new, more effective, more adaptive kinds of compromise formations are instituted.

(1987, pp. 75, 86)

Apart from the evident interaction between different 'schools', the awareness of developmental distortions or deficits, as a result of the influence of child analysts such as Anna Freud, Melanie Klein, René Spitz and Margaret Mahler, has had a noticeable impact on what is understood by successful adaptation. For example, as we saw in the previous chapter, Mahler's work with psychotic children has drawn attention to normal processes of separation–individuation (Mahler 1968, Mahler *et al.*, 1975). The achievement in analytic patients of the appropriate capacity to separate and individuate has become absorbed into statements of aims of analytic treatment. A similar influence has been exerted in recent years by the so-called baby-watchers (Sander, 1975; Stern 1977, 1985; Emde, 1988a, 1988b; Lichtenberg, 1983). These have led to greater awareness by analysts of impediments to normal development which have to be taken into account in formulating the possibilities of modifying faulty developmental processes by means of analysis.

For some analysts the repair of developmental defects (e.g. for the Kohutians through transmuting internalisation) is regarded as possible, while for others the treatment aims have to be modified in order to get the 'best psychological conditions for the functions of the ego' (Freud, 1937a). In the latter case, the assumption is that the essential developmental defects cannot themselves be modified, but that ways of functioning can be developed that assist the individual to cope, both internally and externally. Sandler (1988), in considering the limitations to the efficacy of psychoanalytic therapy, comments:

There seems little doubt, from all the evidence available, that inherited and constitutional differences between individuals are extremely important. They constitute what Freud referred to in 1937 as the underlying 'bedrock', which he saw as placing a biological limitation on what can be achieved. . . . If the findings and formulations [of the baby watchers] . . . are taken seriously then we can formulate our notion of the underlying 'bedrock' in our patients as a *specific* psychobiological bedrock which involves, to very large degree, the structures created by the *specific* individual's development within the *specific* reciprocal relation between the person and his environment – in particular as a result of the infant-caregiver interaction. This certainly puts a limit on what analysis can achieve . . .

(1988, p. 341)

107

The situation has been characterised by Sidney Pulver as follows:

> As a result of the explosion of our knowledge about infant development (Emde, 1988a,b; Kramer & Akhtar, 1988), the view has gained ground that, under optimal therapeutic conditions, therapeutic change can be seen as a kind of new development, analogous to the emotional development of infancy. . . . The implication of this view is that the faulty development which took place is thereby obliterated and replaced by more adaptive functioning. Others, in contrast, hold that the development represented by therapeutic change takes place alongside of, rather than replacing, faulty early development. The analyst attempts to increase the patient's tolerance for his infantile phantasies, not expecting to replace the original developmental paths and the phantasies that were involved in them. Instead, he hopes that the patient, as he becomes more tolerant of his early phantasies, will become more accepting of himself and more able to change his thinking and behaviour. Put differently, the past unconscious is out of reach of the analytic process. Its derivatives intrude into the present unconscious in the form of the transference (Sandler & Sandler, 1983), and this allows for new adaptations of the psyche in the present.
>
> (1991, pp. 84–85)

The persisting awareness of limiting factors in psychoanalytic treatment has significant implications for the conceptualisation of aims. It is less and less appropriate to regard every patient as potentially completely analysable. If we regard development as involving progressive psychobiological adaptation, it could be said that some pathological adaptations can become autonomous, removed from the specific conflicts which brought them into being, and therefore cannot be undone through analysis. This view is shared by Robert Wallerstein, who had been concerned since the 1950s with research into the effectiveness of psychoanalytic treatment. In discussing the changes which have occurred over the years in regard to aims (Wallerstein, 1992), he has reconsidered his own significant paper on 'The goals of psychoanalysis' (1965), and concludes, on the basis of the Psychotherapy Research Project of the Menninger Foundation, which compared the process and outcome in psychoanalysis and psychotherapy (Wallerstein, 1986), that in the 'modern' climate, idealisation and perfectionism in regard to psychoanalysis have been forgone. He says that 'we have come through a rather prolonged era in psychoanalytic thinking . . . of expanding ambitions for the most reconstructive (of character as well as of symptom malfunctioning) psychological therapy yet devised, to a now tempered, realistically much more modest assessment of realisable expectations' (1992, p. 90).

The interaction between the different approaches in the 1980s and 1990s has led to the insight that aims depend on complex intrapsychic and interpersonal processes which can be conceptualised in ways which reflect different theoretical emphases. Cooper remarks on the issues in a more general way.

> It is conceivable that the end of the 1980s, in psychoanalysis as in the 'real world', may mark the end of several of our own cold wars. Our previously relatively orderly theoretical borders, once forming an iron curtain that was impervious to ideas from 'the other side', now seem permeable and even welcoming. The tenacious maintenance of certain theoretical and political boundaries – our Berlin walls, if you wish – that seemed so important until recently, and that has been the source of friction and battle for decades, has seemed increasingly quixotic rather than scientific; perhaps this will lead to an era of greater psychoanalytic cooperation and discourse, if not harmony. As in the 'real world', this peace may be accompanied by enormous confusion and a period of disorderly growth and perhaps regression, as we attempt to adapt to new circumstances.
>
> (1991, p. 107)

At the end of the 1980s a shift of emphasis in regard to the discussion of aims was noticeable in two areas. On the one hand there was a heightened consciousness of the significance of research into the outcome of psychoanalytic treatment, while on the other the differentiation of psychoanalysis from psychoanalytic psychotherapy received increased attention. These concerns were reflected in a series of panel discussions of the American Psychoanalytic Association, held between 1986 and 1990,[8] and we can identify a number of factors which were affecting the formulation of psychoanalytic aims at that time. The medical dominance of psychoanalysis in the United States was being threatened by demands, backed by lawsuits,

---

8 The panels were on the topics of 'The evaluation of outcome of psychoanalytic treatment: should followup by the analyst be part of the post-termination phase of analytic treatment?' (reported by Johan, 1989); 'Changing psychic structure through treatment' (reported by Nersessian, 1989); and three panels on 'Psychoanalysis and psychoanalytic psychotherapy – similarities and differences'. The first of these was on 'Therapeutic technique' (reported by Morris, 1992), the second on 'Indications, contraindications and initiation' (reported by McNutt, 1992), and the third on 'A conceptual overview' (reported by Hoch, 1992). These were followed by two further panels, one on 'The difference between termination in psychotherapy and psychoanalysis' (reported by Becker, 1993), and the other on 'Stability of gains achieved during analytic treatment from a followup perspective' (reported by Martin, 1993).

from various non-medical analytic organisations for admission to the International Psychoanalytical Association. This demand for recognition, which was accepted at the International Congress in Montreal in 1987, was seen as an economic threat by many members of the American Psychoanalytic Association. In addition to this there was a great increase in the number of non-medical psychoanalysts who, while not practising psychoanalysis, were undertaking therapy which was heavily influenced by psychoanalysis – indeed, many psychoanalysts had participated in the training of these psychotherapists. Possibly of greater importance was the awareness that insurance companies and other sources of 'third party' payments were increasingly reluctant to dispense large sums of money for full psychoanalytic treatment, in the absence of substantial proof of its effectiveness.

It is natural that dispensers of 'third party' payments should want to satisfy themselves about the efficacy of the therapies for which they were paying. Such concerns led to the setting up of a number of outcome studies aimed at measuring the effectiveness of psychoanalysis. We can note the Menninger Foundation Psychotherapy Study (extensively described by Wallerstein, 1986), those conducted by Schlessinger and Robbins (1974), the Penn Psychotherapy Study (Luborsky *et al.*, 1988), the reports by Pfeffer (1961, 1963b) and, more recently, Kantrowitz *et al.* (1989) and Bachrach *et al.* (1991). Unfortunately the field abounds with methodological problems. The issue of *how* outcome can be measured became extremely important, as it was clear that empirical studies making use of operationalised criteria (that is, those in which the methods of measurement or observation are precisely spelled out) were necessary if the value of psychoanalysis as a therapeutic method was to be satisfactorily established. All this has focused the minds of analysts on the problem of analytic outcome, and the relation of outcome and aims to psychoanalytic theory and technique.

Because of the difficulty of agreeing on acceptable criteria of outcome and their measurement, the tendency to state aims in terms of intrapsychic changes, which had increased in the 1980s, was further elaborated and reinforced. It had been obvious since the early days of psychoanalysis that the method was not always very effective in removing symptoms, and that the criteria of improvement (which inevitably had an effect on formulations regarding aims) are not necessarily reflected in the disappearance of symptoms. What could now be seen was an extension of the idea of the internalisation of the psychoanalytic *process* to the post-analytic or posttermination phase; there was heightened interest in processes occurring in this phase, in the ways in which post-analytic contact with the analyst affected the patient, and the relevance of this to the assessment of outcome.

It is abundantly clear that the issues of outcome assessment and the differentiation of psychoanalysis from psychoanalytic psychotherapy came more into the foreground of discussion, and tended to be dealt with via formulations about the aims of treatment. Edward Weinshel is reported as saying, in the context of a panel discussion of the differences between psychoanalysis and psychoanalytic psychotherapy, that

> in psychoanalysis there is a clear goal of helping the patient establish an internalised psychoanalytic process with increased capacity for more effective and more objective self-awareness. . . . In contrast, the goals of psychotherapy are usually more in the direction of symptom relief than character change and self-analytic capacity . . . there is less focus on developing an internalised psychoanalytic process and more focus on symptoms, specific goals, and time limits. . . . Termination in psychotherapy is more arbitrary and more linked to subjective improvement than to attainment of an internalised process no longer requiring input from the analyst.
>
> (Morris, 1992, pp. 216–217)

In the same panel the points made by Weinshel are echoed by other contributors. So, for example, David Levy is reported as saying of psychoanalysis (in contrast to psychotherapy) that

> the patient's and analyst's repetitive opportunities to confront and work through transference resistances is a unique path to gaining, with conviction, an understanding and appreciation of the value of an introspective process that continues after termination. Such an occurrence is not a goal and only a rare outcome of psychotherapy.
>
> (Morris, 1992, p. 220)

Throughout all the discussions quoted we find what is to some extent a new development in differentiating psychoanalysis from psychotherapy, that is, a focusing on the question of aims rather than on method and technique. Remarks made by Cooper (reported by Becker, 1993) illustrate this.

> One of the features distinguishing some psychotherapies from some analyses is the difference in the patient's internalisation of the therapist and the process. The psychotherapy patient often remembers the treatment vividly as retaining an objective quality, an event rather than an experience. The analytic patient often remembers the treatment poorly. The latter reflects not only the lesser specificity of goals, but, in successful analyses, reflects the greater degree of internalisation. Whereas psychotherapy patients may, after the treatment, have the therapist as an available introject, and ask themselves what their therapist would have said about something, analytic patients are more likely to have internalised the analyst as an available part of

themselves, and their own behaviours are more integrated. Presumably this is what we mean by structural change, a change of self-representation.

(1993, p. 768)

This approach does not, of course, solve the problem of differentiation between analysis and psychotherapy, as twice or three times weekly psychoanalytic psychotherapy may have precisely the same goals and the same methods as those which have been spelled out for psychoanalysis 'proper', which is normally carried out on a basis of four or five sessions per week. It is often said that the essential difference lies in the frequency of the sessions, and in the assumed effects of this on the treatment process. However, comparisons are difficult, particularly as there is no clear definition of what constitutes psychoanalytic psychotherapy. The latter term can be used to refer to a procedure carried out by a psychoanalyst, in which the patient is seen less than four times a week, or sitting up rather than lying on the couch. It can also refer to the treatment offered by psychotherapists who have not received full psychoanalytic training, but who have had an analysis and have been trained – at least in part – by psychoanalysts; and there are those therapists who have not been analysed but who see the psychoanalytic approach as the basis of their psychotherapeutic work.

To conclude . . .

Weinshel and Renik (1991) provide an appropriate conclusion for this chapter. They say:

> The last ten years have seen a movement, overall, away from categorical insistence on staunch psychoanalytic propositions and toward increasing self-inquiry: we analysts appear more comfortable in acknowledging the limits of what we do know and the tentative nature of many of our established formulations. This greater tolerance for uncertainty suggests, by implication, an underlying increase in genuine confidence regarding the reliable achievements of psychoanalytic understanding. . . . As we hesitantly surrender our illusions concerning the perfectly conducted analysis and the perfect analytic outcome, we also relinquish the phantasy of a crystal clear distinction between psychoanalysis and psychoanalytic psychotherapy. In the last ten years, we have become considerably less definitive and less certain about what a psychoanalytic result is and how a psychoanalytic treatment should be carried out.

(1991, pp. 13, 21)

9

A framework for thinking about aims

The literature on aims, from Freud to the present day, reflects a variety of views and formulations which clearly cannot be brought together into a single definition. To some degree the discussion of aims has been complicated because over the years psychoanalysts have displayed a remarkable reluctance to discard previously held theoretical concepts, and many statements regarding the aims of psychoanalysis appear and reappear in different theoretical and historical contexts. This conservative tendency is probably one of the reasons that the development of the theory of aims has not proceeded in a straight line, and there is a rather erratic and slow progression in the theory, in which there is constant repetition of previous formulations as well as the evolution of new ideas. It is striking how closely the history of the conceptualisation of aims reflects the history of psychoanalysis itself, affected as this history has been by the prevailing paradigm, the attitudes of the public, and of the general psychiatric–psychological community and its institutions.

As noted in our introduction, we have based our study of aims on a historical approach. It has become abundantly clear that there is no single way of formulating the concept of aims, and that we are dealing with a multifaceted problem. There has been an awareness of this in the literature on the subject, and in the preceding chapters we have seen this reflected in the attempts made to create categories or 'levels' of aims. So, distinctions have been made, for example, between process and outcome goals (e.g. Wallerstein, 1965), between treatment and life goals (Ticho, 1972), and between proximate and ultimate goals (e.g. Glueck, 1960). Such attempts at distinction, which have arisen in specific contexts, have been extremely useful, but suffer the disadvantage that to some extent they compartmentalise the field, do not do justice to its great complexity, and are anchored to the theoretical ideas prevailing at the time. Accordingly, we decided to approach the problem of conceptualising aims by first considering the different *perspectives* from which the issues could be viewed. In order to do this we have re-examined the main trends in the psycho-analytic literature. The perspectives considered below are certainly not independent of one another, and there is significant overlap. Each is neither simple nor unidimensional but has different aspects to varying degrees. Consider, for a moment, the frequently stated formulation that the aim of analysis is to bring about structural change. Yet the meaning of such a statement will be dependent on whether it is looked at from the point of view of, for instance, ego psychology, self psychology or object-relations theory; moreover, we would have to ask which structure is involved. Is change being considered in relation to superego, ego, mental representations or relations to internal objects?

Freud put forward several different approaches to the problem of aims. First and foremost was, of course, the therapeutic aim, i.e., of curing the patient of the symptoms or illness that brought him to analysis. But this essentially medical perspective caused a problem because Freud was to see that symptoms did not always disappear, and as a consequence conceived of the analytic process as differentiated from the therapeutic goal: the aim of analysis became rather to apply the method – in short, to analyse – and by the application of this method, *cure* was seen as a (hoped-for) byproduct of analysis as a method of *research* which had to be conducted without any specific goal, except that of making what is unconscious conscious and acceptable to the patient. Nevertheless, the therapeutic aim was not discarded, but the method, involving relative 'goallessness', was seen as being potentially curative. This point of view, of the 'conjunction' between research and therapy, has persisted throughout the subsequent development of psychoanalysis, both in its original form and as a distinction between 'analytically satisfactory' and 'therapeutically satisfactory' outcomes of the analytic work; and indeed there are many analysts who stoutly defend the view that the aim of analysis is to analyse, and that 'cure' is a byproduct. We believe that this view has an understandable defensive function, in that it serves as a protection from all the problems associated with defining the aim of the analytic work, and reinforces the boundary between psychoanalysis and psychoanalytic psychotherapy.

In the preceding chapters we have documented a multitude of statements about the aims of psychoanalytic treatment. These have ranged from abstract metapsychological statements to relatively concrete goals related to the individual's mode of functioning in his personal and professional life. Weinshel (1990) had characterised the previous thirty-five years of psychoanalytic theory and practice as a 'gradual movement toward a more modest conceptualisation of psychoanalysis', and he lists a number of significant changes which indicate 'the extent to which our claims have become increasingly realistic and significantly more in harmony with our clinical observations' (p. 280). We can extract from Weinshel's formulations the following implications for aims: psychoanalytic 'cures' are rarely spoken of. Psychic conflict cannot be completely eliminated, nor is the idea maintained that a 'complete' analysis is possible. Transferences cannot be completely eliminated or resolved. While insight is aimed for, it is no longer regarded as an absolutely necessary requirement, without which the analysis cannot proceed. The retrieval of repressed childhood memories is no longer the main aim of the analytic work. On the other hand, over the years, analysis is now regarded as aiming at bringing about intrapsychic changes which would result in improved resolution of the patient's main conflicts. While analyses are never complete, and transference can never be completely resolved, the analysis can still be seen as successful. Instead of aiming at insight, attainment of the capacity for self-observation is to be aimed for.

For each of these goals, and indeed for all analytic goals given in the literature, we can ask: why should we as analysts want to achieve this particular aim with a particular patient? Why should we, for example, want to make the unconscious conscious? The answer must inevitably be some sort of formulation in terms of attaining improved mental health, and indeed many of the outcome goals listed in the literature can – and have been – taken, in one way or another, to be indicators of mental health. It could be (and has been) argued that a satisfactory statement of aim would be 'to broaden the intellectual horizons of the patient'. The response to the 'why?' question might then be that the analysis would only be offered to patients who want to achieve this aim. This approach is maintained by some psychoanalysts who, nevertheless, offer analysis to patients who come for treatment in order to find relief from their symptoms. As we shall see, the stance that the analyst can work independently of the aim to cure is incorrect. Yet it is generally agreed nowadays that the very concept of mental health is embedded in a particular socio-cultural context with its own specific value system. (Of course, some conditions – e.g. severe depression or obsessional neurosis – can be regarded as pathological irrespective of the culture in which they are found.)

Consider, for instance, the following definition given by Karl Menninger (quoted by Jahoda):

> Let us define mental health as the adjustment of human beings to the world and to each other with a maximum of effectiveness and happiness. Not just efficiency, or just contentment – or the grace of obeying the rules of the game cheerfully. It is all of this together. It is the ability to maintain an even temper, an alert intelligence, socially considerate behaviour, and a happy disposition. This, I think, is a healthy mind.
>
> (Jahoda, 1958, p. 18)

We shall make no comment, but it is clear that the concept of mental health involves, implicitly or explicitly, a picture of man, as well as a *Weltanschauung*. Societal values influence our concepts of mental health – so, for example, we might think of the influence of changing views on homosexuality, on delinquency in children and adolescents, on toilet training, and, last but not least, on the role of women in society. In the light of society's current expectations many psychoanalysts would now assess mental health very differently from the way in which such an assessment might have been made two or three decades previously.

Roy Schafer (1994), in an essay on Heinz Hartmann's *Psychoanalysis and Moral Values* (1960), says that

> the moral implications of the definition of 'health' are themselves open to critical scrutiny. 'Health' may be regarded as an idea replete with moral values that control it both as an idea and a practice. Out of recognition of the constant play of power in human relations, one may therefore ask: whose ideas of health are we talking about, and what are its assumptions? Whose health should matter? How much of what we call health is to be pursued, and what are the social consequences of that? There are many more questions of that sort. . . . As in our society at large, so in psychoanalysis, we encounter many varied presuppositions about what is health, who is healthy, whose health matters, and whose judgment counts. These variations imply variations in values.
>
> (1994, p. 275)

From the earliest days of psychoanalysis it has been abundantly clear that it is inappropriate simply to speak of the attainment of mental health or normality as an aim of psychoanalytic therapy. One has only to recall Freud's comment to a hypothetical patient that 'much will be gained if we succeed in transforming your hysterical misery into common unhappiness' (1895, p. 305), and the limitations to the effectiveness of psychoanalytic treatment described by Freud in 'Analysis terminable and interminable' (1937a).

Throughout the psychoanalytic literature after Freud we find a growing concern with the problem of what analysis can achieve in any individual patient. The views expressed range from highly idealised 'pie-in-the-sky' formulations to emphasis on realistic and pragmatic conceptions, taking into account what is possible rather than ideal. We can contrast, for example, the aim of removing a sexual perversion with the aim of enabling the patient to live with it without getting into trouble and without damaging himself or others; indeed, an activity which had, in past years, been labelled as a perversion may nowadays not be regarded as a perversion at all.

With the realisation that *general* aims cannot be formulated in blanket fashion for all patients, a need has been felt to consider aims in terms of

116

their appropriateness in regard to individual patients. The increasing awareness of the limitations of the psychoanalytic method has brought to the fore the question of *specific* aims for specific patients. The difficulties in specifying general aims, put in terms of mental health for any individual patient, have been substantial. Mental health formulations have usually been put in terms of *observables* such as the disappearance of symptoms,[1] but have also been described as sexual and social fulfilment, improvement in the capacity for work, and the like. This was clearly unsatisfactory, and from early in the history of psychoanalysis stimulated attempts to define aims by formulating the outcome of treatment in general *metapsychological* terms – analysis aims at lessening the harshness of the superego, promoting the autonomy of the ego, improving control of instinctual impulses, increasing the capacity for sublimation, etc. Such definitions of aim have been described much more precisely than the global 'mental health' aims, but they are, of course, embedded in the particular theoretical model being used by the author. So we find the aim of 'making the unconscious conscious' put forward as an aim in the framework of Freud's topographical theory; 'where id was, there ego shall be' is a formulation within his structural theory; 'attaining increased autonomy of the ego' is a product of post-Freudian ego psychology; achieving greater 'coherence of the self' is an aim proposed by the self psychologists; 'working through the depressive position' or the withdrawal of projections are postulated by Kleinian theorists; and so on. These differences are not only reflections of differences in theoretical language, but may represent substantial, and even incompatible, differences in basic theoretical conceptions, and thus in ideas about appropriate aims.

Clearly the formulation of aims in terms of 'outcome' goals, whether or not put in terms of observables or metapsychology, has not solved the problem of finding a suitable general formulation of aims. Consequently there have been consistent attempts to approach the task by focusing on the psychoanalytic process itself and on 'process' goals, beginning with the formulation of aims at the diagnostic stage,[2] and ending with those relating to the termination of the analysis. In this context a distinction has been made between proximate and ultimate (or distant) goals. To recall Glueck (1960) again: ultimate goals are to help the patient to gain 'self understanding, self realisation and self acceptance', while proximate goals are

---

[1] In his classic description of different categories of aims, Wallerstein (1965) restricts outcome goals to observable behaviour and changes in relationships. We use the term in the extended sense, including the internal changes postulated as goals of psychoanalytic treatment.

[2] We can recall Ernst Ticho's remark (1972) that every diagnosis implies a prognosis, and every prognosis implies a treatment aim.

those immediately achieved in the psychoanalytic situation, and if achieved would enable the patient to get to know the dynamisms of unconscious motivation and emotions. To complicate the issue, psychoanalysts have been aware that the aims of psychoanalytic therapy have not necessarily been achieved at the time the analysis ends. The criteria for the termination of an analysis and the achievement of the goals of the analysis are manifestly not identical. There has always been a notion of 'post-analytic improvement', with the assumption that processes begun during the analysis will continue after the analysis has ended.

Treatment goals are inextricably related to the 'life goals' of the patient and, we would add, to the life goals of the analyst. Such life goals are both conscious and unconscious, and to the extent to which the analyst's and the patient's goals are the same, they may provide a mutually accepted value system within which the analysis is conducted. So, for example, if both analyst and patient place a high value on economic success, or on having children, as outcome goals, such shared values will undoubtedly affect the course of the analysis. Incidentally, it is worth noting in this connection that there is increasing evidence that the personality 'fit' between analyst and patient is a crucial factor in determining the outcome of treatment, indicating the importance of the interaction between the two specific persons involved (see, for example, Kantrowitz *et al.*, 1989).

At first sight it is tempting to consider the analyst's conscious and unconscious value systems, insofar as they affect the analysis, as countertransference; but what do we mean by countertransference? In the introduction to this book it was suggested that countertransference could usefully be considered as the specific response of the analyst to his specific patient. This view of countertransference specifically excludes general features of the analyst's personality, and accordingly would also exclude the analyst's particular socially and culturally determined sets of values. Yet they are deeply involved in the transactions which take place in the analytic encounter, and need to be scrutinised just as much as those reactions which are normally regarded as countertransferential. But there is an inevitable limit to this scrutiny, and there is a basic core of values which enters as conscious or unconscious 'givens' in the analysis; and this only comes under scrutiny when a conflict of values between analyst and patient arises. It may be tempting to see such a conflict as an expression of the patient's resistance when in fact it is not, and it may be more appropriate for the analyst to think in terms of a value-system-based countertransference reaction.

While the complexity of discussions about aims testifies to the richness of psychoanalytic theory and practice, it also points to the lack of precision in regard to the conceptualisation of aims. How best, then, to approach this problem? It is useful, we believe, to look first at the different perspectives from which the problem of aims can be viewed, and group them under at least three main headings.

The *historical-conceptual perspective* includes the examination of aims from the point of view of the phases of theoretical development in psycho-analysis and the various 'schools' of psychoanalytic thought – e.g. the topographical and structural models, ego psychology, self psychology, object-relations theory, and the Kleinian school.

The *socio-cultural perspective* approaches aims from the point of view of mental health and normality within a particular societal context. It also encompasses considerations of the effectiveness of psychoanalytic therapy and its cost-effectiveness. The aspect of cost-effectiveness has become particularly important as a consequence of the lowering of funding for analysis by insurance companies and other agencies, in those countries that maintain such schemes.

The *clinical and technical perspective* relates to such issues as the distinction between ideal and realisable goals, between general and specific goals, between tactical proximate (process) goals and strategic distant (outcome) goals, between the conscious goals and unconscious goals of both patient and analyst; and between what is attainable during the analysis and what is aimed for in terms of post-analytic change.

In the light of these perspectives we shall consider some of the processes occurring in the mind of the analyst from the point of his initial assessment of the patient to the end of the analysis. Before seeing the patient the analyst has a whole spectrum of possible 'aims' in his mind – a reservoir of aims, so to speak. Some, but not all of these, will be conscious, others unconscious but available to consciousness, and a significant number will be inaccessible without a great deal of self-analytic work on the part of the analyst. The analyst's unconscious countertransference and the unconscious treatment aims may be closely intertwined. So, for example, the analyst may have an unconscious wish to change the patient's sexual orientation or to have him succeed academically or (especially in the case of a training analyst) to turn the patient into a substitute son or daughter.

When the analyst meets a patient for the first time, the whole range of his ideas about aims will be, consciously or unconsciously, at his disposal.[3] In his first contact with the patient he will not only become aware of the

---

[3] To the extent that aims may enter into the criteria for differentiating psychoanalysis from psychoanalytic psychotherapy (see Chapter 8), it would be of interest to explore whether the *range* of aims in the mind of the psychotherapist is for practical purposes more restricted than in the psychoanalyst. The question can also be posed of whether the psychotherapist has more conscious awareness of outcome goals than the psycho-analyst normally has.

119

patient's conscious reasons for wanting an analysis, and the ideas the patient has of the changes he hopes will result from it, but he may also have an idea of the patient's unconscious analytic aims. The analyst will (sometimes quite automatically) make an assessment, to the extent that he can, of the patient's personality, psychopathology, mental structure, and his suitability for analysis. Undoubtedly all these elements have an impact on the analyst's (conscious or unconscious) ideas of changes which he regards as *feasible* goals in the work *with that particular patient*. We can say that even in the analyst's initial contact with the patient, the relation between his inner spectrum of aims and what is feasible automatically modifies the range of possible treatment aims in regard to the patient; and the selection of aims will be different from one patient to another. It is important to emphasise that such a progressive selection will occur even if the analyst does not consciously formulate ideas about the aims of treatment for the patient, and even if the analyst consciously subscribes to the view that the analyst should have no aims for the analysis apart from that of applying the analytic method. It is normal analytic practice for the analyst to refrain from expressing any ideas about the aims of the analysis to the patient, or to give any indication or promise that analysis will bring about some specific change in the patient. On the other hand, it is usual practice to indicate that analysis might help the patient in regard to his complaints by attaining greater understanding of himself.

During the initial phase of the analysis it is likely that the analyst's concern will be with process or proximate goals, as the analyst is primarily concerned with assisting the patient to enter fully into analysis, and to deal with the patient's initial anxieties and resulting resistances. As the analysis progresses, and the possibilities for change in the patient become clearer, thoughts may arise about aimed-for internal changes – for example lessening of pathological guilt and shame, and increased tolerance for feelings such as envy, grief, love or hate. Similarly ideas about desirable external manifestations of change, such as the disappearance of phobic symptoms, increase in the capacity to work more productively and enjoyably, etc., come more to the fore in the analyst's mind. But although such outcome goals may enter the scene, process goals are not put aside, and are involved in relation to all interventions made by the analyst throughout the analysis. Thus any interpretation involves an implicit process goal in that the analyst is aiming to bring about a tolerance in the patient of what was unconscious and defended against, and with it a lessening of conflict. Throughout, the analyst will of necessity take into account the reality of the patient's intrapsychic and other limitations, and this awareness will inevitably have repercussions on the aims of the analytic work. The analytic process is one in which the analyst has to be ready to change aims – to shift gears, so to speak – as the work proceeds. Such change relates not only to process goals, but to outcome goals. On the side of the patient there are changes in the aim of the analysis as well, for the patient's life goals may well change during the course of the analysis. In all of this there is a mutual interaction between patient and analyst, with the aims of the analysis being influenced in both parties through the moment-to-moment interpersonal interaction in the analytic situation.

When the question of termination arises, in the mind of the patient or the analyst, or in both, outcome goals become more prominent. As criteria for termination are being considered by the analyst, so he will increasingly take into account the realities of the patient's state and situation. As we have seen, the literature on termination has shown a growing awareness among analysts that the idea of the fully analysed analysand is quite inappropriate. The essential criterion for termination (from the side of the analyst) seems to be the gaining of an affirmative answer to the question, 'Can the patient, with all his limitations and peculiarities, in the reality situation in which he finds himself, manage more or less successfully without further analysis?' Of course, this formulation leaves the question of what is meant by 'managing more or less successfully'. We suggest that the criteria are established through the intercommunication and dialogue between patient and analyst. Such a view has led to the recommendation that no analysis should be regarded as completed, but rather as interrupted, and that an 'open-door' policy be adopted by the analyst, so that the patient can return for a further 'tranche' of analysis. Emphasis has been placed over the years on the development of the 'self-analytic function' which allows the analysis to progress after termination. In addition, one can say that in successful analytic cases much of what has previously been conscious insight will, with its continued application, become automatic and will operate below the level of consciousness.

By now the reader may well ask: 'But what are the aims of psycho-analysis? Why should one undertake such an arduous task?' Our answer has to be that there is no *one* answer. All the many answers to this hypothetical question are to be found in the statements about aims in the chapters of this book, for *all* are valid – but they are valid at different times, in different contexts and from different perspectives; but it is always appropriate to specify the *perspective* from which a particular formulation of analytic aims is viewed. We have emphasised the differences in regard to mental health in different patients, and how the formulation of aims will vary according to the value systems of analyst and patient. Earlier we pointed out that if we applied the 'why' question to any one of the statements analysts have made about the aims of analysis, we inevitably end up with an answer which, broadly speaking, can be considered to be in the area of 'mental health'. The reader might now, quite legitimately, ask what we mean by 'mental health', and the answer we would give would be this. Mental health, like aims themselves, can be defined as an essentially multi-dimensional 'elastic' notion (see Sandler, 1983), embracing a very large number of criteria, so large that they probably could not, in the present state of our knowledge, be fully enumerated. We have described how, during the course of an analysis, patient and analyst work towards a selection of mental health criteria which represent a state of 'mental health' *specific to the patient in his particular life situation*, taking into account all his personal limitations and peculiarities, as well as his socio-cultural context. For one patient it may be predominantly to get on better with colleagues; for another it may be primarily to be less self-damaging; for a third it may be to overcome a working inhibition. What this state of 'mental health' will be at the end of the analysis cannot be predetermined, but will be the product of the interaction and what can be considered to be the continual conscious and unconscious negotiation between the two partners in the analytic enterprise.

In the light of the arguments we have put forward it would follow that a desirable outcome of analysis will vary from one patient to another, and is not capable of being encompassed by one definition or measured by one single criterion. It would seem that outcome studies in the area of psychoanalysis need to take individual differences into account, as the outcome of a successful analysis for one person may be very different from the outcome of a successful analysis for another. One way of doing this is through a specific form of empirical research which does not require any special apparatus, apart from the minds of those analysts who participate in the research. In a sense it represents a very psychoanalytical approach, one which has worked well in the study of other concepts. An example is a study of the concept of psychic trauma as it exists in the minds of analysts and utilised in their practice, conducted at the Sigmund Freud Institute in Frankfurt (Sandler *et al.*, 1987; 1991). What such a research method involves, besides historical and theoretical clarification of the concept, is the formation of a research group of analysts who meet regularly, and discuss the analytic process in their patients from the point of view of aims which they focus on at any stage in the work with specific patients. Whenever a process goal is mentioned, the 'why' question should be asked, and continue to be asked until a particular latent outcome goal becomes manifest; and these outcome goals have to be as specific as possible. Psychoanalysts work with implicit constructs and 'private' theories, which do not always correspond to accepted or 'public' theories, and the approach suggested may elicit the implicit working models of the analyst. The results of such an approach may be very surprising and illuminating, allowing for advances in theory. For such a project to be successful, certain conditions have to be fulfilled. For example the members of the group have to trust one another, and they must not feel that their ambitions within their analytic society or institute are threatened, or that their professional status as analysts is at risk if they do not conform to a particular orthodoxy or school. Depending on the outcome of such a study, the next step might be to attempt to trace connections between specific process goals and outcome goals; and if this yields results, both psychoanalysis and applied psychoanalysis in the form of psychoanalytic psychotherapy may profit. But in any case, this approach may lead to a useful frame of reference which may allow communication between analysts about aims to be more precise, may reduce vagueness, arbitrariness and, above all, idealisation in discussions about what analysis can aim to achieve.

References

Alexander, F. (1925) 'A metapsychological description of the process of cure'. *International Journal of Psycho-Analysis*, 6: 13–34.

—— (1954a) 'Some quantitative aspects of psychoanalytic technique'. *Journal of the American Psychoanalytic Association*, 2: 685–701.

—— (1954b) 'Psychoanalysis and psychotherapy'. *Journal of the American Psychoanalytic Association*, 2: 722–733.

—— and French, T. (1946) *Psychoanalytic Therapy*. New York: Ronald Press.

Altman, L.L. (1964) (reporter) Panel: 'Theory of psychoanalytic therapy'. *Journal of the American Psychoanalytic Association*, 12: 620–631.

Arlow, J.A. (1987) 'The dynamics of interpretation'. *Psychoanalytic Quarterly*, 56: 68–87.

—— and Brenner, C. (1964) *Psychoanalytic Concepts and the Structural Theory*. New York: International Universities Press.

Bachrach, H.M., Galatzer-Levy, R., Skolnikoff, A. and Waldron, S. (1991) 'On the efficacy of psychoanalysis'. *Journal of the American Psychoanalytic Association*, 39: 871–916.

Bader, M.J. (1994) 'The tendency to neglect therapeutic aims in psychoanalysis'. *Psychoanalytic Quarterly*, 63: 246–270.

Baker, R. (1993) 'The patient's discovery of the psychoanalyst as a new object'. *International Journal of Psycho-Analysis*, 74: 1223–1233.

Balint, M. (1932) 'Character analysis and new beginning'. In: *Primary Love and Psychoanalytic Technique*. London: Hogarth Press, 1950, pp. 159–173.

—— (1935) 'The final goal of psychoanalytical treatment'. In: *Primary Love and Psychoanalytic Technique*. London: Hogarth Press, 1952, pp. 188–199.

—— (1950) 'On the termination of analysis'. *International Journal of Psycho-Analysis*, 31: 196–199.

—— (1952) *Primary Love and Psychoanalytic Technique*. London: Hogarth Press.

Barchilon, J. (1956) 'On countertransference "cures" '. *Journal of the American Psychoanalytic Association*, 6: 222–236.

Becker, T.C. (1993) (reporter) Panel: 'The difference between termination in psychotherapy and psychoanalysis'. *Journal of the American Psychoanalytic Association*, 41: 765–773.

Bergler, E. (1937) 'Symposium on the theory of therapeutic results of psychoanalysis'. *International Journal of Psycho-Analysis*, 18: 146–160.

Bernstein, I. (1956) 'Indications and goals of child analysis as compared with child psychotherapy'. *Journal of the American Psychoanalytic Association*, 4: 158–163.

Bibring, E. (1937) 'Symposium on the theory of therapeutic results of psychoanalysis'. *International Journal of Psycho-Analysis*, 18: 170–189.

—— (1954) 'Psychoanalysis and the dynamic psychotherapies'. *Journal of the American Psychoanalytic Association*, 2: 745–770.

Bion, W. (1954) 'Notes on the theory of schizophrenia'. *International Journal of Psycho-Analysis*, 35: 113–118.

—— (1970) *Attention and Interpretation*. London: Tavistock.

Blum, H. (1994) *Reconstruction in Psychoanalysis: Childhood Revisited and Recreated*. Madison, CT: International Universities Press.

Brenner, C. (1976) *Psychoanalytic Technique and Psychic Conflict*. New York: International Universities Press.

—— (1994) 'The mind as conflict and compromise formation'. *Journal of Clinical Psychoanalysis*, 3: 473–488.

Bridger, H. (1950) 'Criteria for the termination of analysis'. *International Journal of Psycho-Analysis*, 31: 202–203.

Buxbaum, E. (1950) 'Technique of terminating analysis'. *International Journal of Psycho-Analysis*, 31: 184–190.

Chessick, R. (1993) *A Dictionary for Psychotherapists*. Northvale, NJ: Jason Aronson.

Cooper, A.M. (1985) 'A historical view of psychoanalytic paradigms'. In: A. Rothstein (ed.) *Models of the Mind: Their Relationships to Clinical Work*. Madison, CT: International Universities Press, pp. 5–20.

—— (1987) 'The transference neurosis: a concept ready for retirement'. *Psychoanalytic Inquiry*, 7: 569–585.

—— (1989) 'Concepts of therapeutic effectiveness in psychoanalysis: a historical review'. *Psychoanalytic Inquiry*, 9: 4–25.

—— (1991) 'Psychoanalysis: the past decade'. *Psychoanalytic Inquiry*, 11: 107–122.

Cramer, B. and Flournoy, O. (1976) (reporters) Panel: 'The changing expectations of patients and psychoanalysts today'. *International Journal of Psycho-Analysis*, 57: 419–427.

Deutsche Psychoanalytische Gesellschaft (eds) (1930) *Zehn Jahre Berliner Psychoanalytisches Institut*. Vienna: Internationaler Psychoanalytischer Verlag (ed. Sándor Rado in cooperation with Otto Fenichel and Carl Müller-Braunschweig).

Eissler, K.R. (1953) 'The effect of the structure of the ego on psychoanalytic technique'. *Journal of the American Psychoanalytic Association*, 1: 104–143.

—— (1963) 'Notes on the psychoanalytic concept of cure'. *Psychoanalytic Study of the Child*, 18: 424–463.

Ellenberger, H.F. (1970) *The Discovery of the Unconscious: The History and Evolution of Dynamic Psychiatry*. New York: Basic Books.

Emde, R.N. (1988a) 'Development terminable and interminable: I. Innate and motivational factors from infancy'. *International Journal of Psycho-Analysis*, 69: 23–42.

—— (1988b) 'Development terminable and interminable: II. Recent psycho-analytic theory and therapeutic considerations'. *International Journal of Psycho-Analysis*, 69: 283–296.

Erikson, E.H. (1950) *Childhood and Society*. New York: W.W. Norton.

Etchegoyen, R.H. (1991a) *The Fundamentals of Psychoanalytic Technique*. London: Karnac Books.

—— (1991b) 'Psychoanalysis during the last decade: clinical and theoretical aspects'. *Psychoanalytic Inquiry*, 11: 88 –106.

Fairbairn, W.R.D. (1954) *An Object Relations Theory of the Personality*. New York: Basic Books.

—— (1958) 'On the nature and aims of psychoanalytical treatment'. *International Journal of Psycho-Analysis*, 39: 374–385.

Fenichel, O. (1934) *Outline of Clinical Psychoanalysis*. New York: W.W. Norton.

—— (1935) 'Zur Theorie der psychoanalytischen Technik'. *Internationale Zeitschrift für Psychoanalyse*, 21: 78–95.

—— (1937) 'Symposium on the theory of therapeutic results of psychoanalysis'. *International Journal of Psycho-Analysis*, 18: 133–138.

—— (1941) *Problems of Psychoanalytic Technique*. New York: The Psychoanalytic Quarterly, Inc.

—— (1945) *The Psychoanalytic Theory of Neurosis*. New York: W.W. Norton.

Ferenczi, S. (1927) 'The problem of the termination of the analysis'. In: *Final Contributions to the Problems and Methods of Psycho-Analysis*. London: Hogarth Press, 1955, pp. 77–86.

—— (1928) 'The elasticity of psychoanalytic technique'. In: *Final Contributions to the Problems and Methods of Psycho-Analysis*. London: Hogarth Press, 1955, pp. 87-101.

—— and Rank, O. (1925) *The Development of Psychoanalysis*. New York and Washington: Nervous and Mental Disease Publishing Company.

Firestein, S.K. (1969) (reporter) Panel: 'Problems of termination in the analysis of adults'. *Journal of the American Psychoanalytic Association*, 17: 222–237.

Freud, A. (1936) *The Ego and the Mechanisms of Defence*. London: Hogarth Press.

—— (1954) 'The widening scope of indications for psychoanalysis: discussion'. *Journal of the American Psychoanalytic Association*, 2: 607–620.

—— (1963) 'The concept of developmental lines'. *The Psychoanalytic Study of the Child*, 18: 245–265.

—— (1965) *Normality and Pathology in Childhood*. New York: International Universities Press.

—— (1976) 'Changes in psychoanalytic practice and experience'. *International Journal of Psycho-Analysis*, 57: 257–260.

Freud, S. (1895) 'The psychotherapy of hysteria', in J. Breuer and S. Freud (1893–5) *Studies on Hysteria. The Standard Edition of the Complete Psychological Works of Sigmund Freud*, ed. James Strachey, 24 volumes, London: Hogarth Press, 1953–73, vol. 2, pp. 253–305.

—— (1896) 'Further remarks on the neuro-psychoses of defence'. *Standard Edition*, 3, pp. 159–185.

—— (1900) *The Interpretation of Dreams*. *Standard Edition*, 4–5.

—— (1904) 'Freud's psychoanalytic procedure'. *Standard Edition*, 7, pp. 249–254.

—— (1905) 'On psychotherapy'. *Standard Edition*, 7, pp. 257–268.

—— (1906) 'Psychoanalysis and the establishment of the facts in legal proceedings'. *Standard Edition*, 9, pp. 97–114.

—— (1909) 'A phobia in a five-year-old boy'. *Standard Edition*, 10, pp. 3–147.

—— (1910) 'The future prospects of psychoanalytic therapy'. *Standard Edition*, 11, pp. 139–151.

—— (1912) 'Recommendations to physicians practising psychoanalysis'. *Standard Edition*, 12, pp. 109–120.

—— (1914) 'On narcissism: an introduction'. *Standard Edition*, 14, pp. 67–102.

—— (1915a) 'Instincts and their vicissitudes'. *Standard Edition*, 14, pp. 109–140.

—— (1915b) 'Repression'. *Standard Edition*, 14, pp. 141–158.

—— (1915c) 'The unconscious'. *Standard Edition*, 14, pp. 159–215.

—— (1916–17) *Introductory Lectures on Psychoanalysis*. *Standard Edition*, 15–16.

—— (1917) 'Mourning and melancholia'. *Standard Edition*, 14, pp. 237–258.

—— (1919) 'Lines of advance in psychoanalytic therapy'. *Standard Edition*, 17, pp. 157–168.

—— (1920) *Beyond the Pleasure Principle*. *Standard Edition*, 18, pp. 3–64.

—— (1922a) 'Two encyclopaedia articles'. *Standard Edition*, 18, pp. 235–259.

—— (1922b) Remarks summarized in: *Bulletin of the IPA*, 1923. *International Journal of Psycho-Analysis*, 4: 358–399.

—— (1923) *The Ego and the Id*. *Standard Edition*, 19, pp. 3–66.

—— (1924) 'Loss of reality in neurosis and psychosis'. *Standard Edition*, 19, pp. 183–187.

—— (1926a) *Inhibitions, Symptoms and Anxiety*. *Standard Edition*, 20, pp. 77–175.

—— (1926b) 'The question of lay analysis'. *Standard Edition*, 20, pp. 179–250.

—— (1927) 'The question of lay analysis: postscript'. *Standard Edition*, 20, pp. 251–258.

—— (1933) *New Introductory Lectures*. *Standard Edition*, 22, pp. 3–182.

—— (1935) 'Letter to the mother of a homosexual'. In: E. Jones, *The Life and Work of Sigmund Freud*, vol. 3. New York: Basic Books, 1957, pp. 195–196.

—— (1937a) 'Analysis terminable and interminable'. *Standard Edition*, 23, pp. 209–253.

—— (1937b) 'Constructions in analysis'. *Standard Edition*, 23, pp. 255–269.

—— (1940) *An Outline of Psychoanalysis*. *Standard Edition*, 23, pp. 141–207.

Fromm-Reichmann, F. (1954) 'Psychoanalytic and general dynamic conceptions of theory and of therapy: differences and similarities'. *Journal of the American Psychoanalytic Association*, 2: 711–772.

Furst, S. (1980) 'Summary and concluding remarks: 31st International Psychoanalytic Congress'. *International Journal of Psycho-Analysis*, 61: 225–236.

Gaskill, H.S. (1980) 'The closing phase of the psychoanalytic treatment of adults and the goals of psychoanalysis, "the myth of perfectibility" '. *International Journal of Psycho-Analysis*, 61: 11–22.

Gay, P. (1988) *Freud: A Life for our Time*. London: J.M. Dent.

Gill, M.M. (1954) 'Psychoanalysis and exploratory psychotherapy'. *Journal of the American Psychoanalytic Association*, 2: 771–797.

—— (1963) *Topography and Systems in Psychoanalytic Theory*. *Psychological Issues*, Monograph 10. New York: International Universities Press.

Gitelson, M. (1951) 'Psychoanalysis and dynamic psychiatry'. *Archives of Neurology and Psychiatry*, 66: 280–288.

—— (1954) 'Therapeutic problems in the analysis of the "normal" candidate'. *International Journal of Psycho-Analysis*, 35: 174–183.

—— (1962) 'The curative factors in the first phase of analysis'. *International Journal of Psycho-Analysis*, 43: 194–205.

Glover, E. (1937) 'Symposium on the theory of therapeutic results of psycho-analysis'. *International Journal of Psycho-Analysis*, 18: 125–132.

—— (1940) *An Investigation of the Technique of Psychoanalysis*. London: Baillière, Tindall & Cox.

—— (1954) 'Therapeutic criteria of psychoanalysis'. *International Journal of Psycho-Analysis*, 35: 95–101.

Glueck, B. (1960) 'Psychoanalysis: reflections and comments'. In: P.H. Hoch and J. Zubin (eds) *Current Approaches to Psychoanalysis*. New York, London: Grune & Stratton, pp. 123–140.

Goldberg, A. (1987) 'Psychoanalysis and negotiation'. *Psychoanalytic Quarterly*, 56: 109–129.

Gray, P. (1965) (reporter) Panel: 'Limitations of psychoanalysis'. *Journal of the American Psychoanalytic Association*, 23: 181–190.

Greenacre, P. (1954) 'The role of transference: practical considerations in relation to psychoanalytic therapy'. *Journal of the American Psychoanalytic Association*, 2: 671–684.

Greenberg, J.R. (1991) *Oedipus and Beyond*. Cambridge, MA: Harvard University Press.

—— and Mitchell, S.A. (1983) *Object Relations in Psychoanalytic Theory*. Cambridge, MA: Harvard University Press.

Greenson, R.R. (1967) *The Technique and Practice of Psychoanalysis*. London: Hogarth Press.

Grinberg, L. (1980) 'The closing phase of the psychoanalytic treatment of adults and the goals of psychoanalysis, "the search for truth about one's self"'. *International Journal of Psycho-Analysis*, 61: 25–37.

Grotjahn, M. (1964) 'Open end technique in psychoanalysis'. *Psychoanalytic Quarterly*, 33: 270–271.

Hartmann, H. (1939a) 'Psychoanalysis and the concept of health'. *International Journal of Psycho-Analysis*, 20: 308–321.

—— (1939b) *Ego Psychology and the Problem of Adaptation*. New York: International Universities Press, 1958.

—— (1960) *Psychoanalysis and Moral Values*. New York: International Universities Press.

Hinshelwood, R.D. (1989) *A Dictionary of Kleinian Thought*. London: Free Association Books.

Hoch, S. (1992) (reporter) Panel: 'Psychoanalysis and psychoanalytic psychotherapy – similarities and differences: a conceptual overview'. *Journal of the American Psychoanalytic Association*, 40: 233–238.

Hoffer, W. (1950) 'Three psychological criteria for the termination of treatment'. *International Journal of Psycho-Analysis*, 31: 194–95.

Horney, K. (1951) 'Ziele der psychoanalytischen Therapie'. *Psyche*, 5: 463–472.

Horowitz, M.J., Kernberg, O. and Weinshel, E.M. (eds) (1993) *Psychic Structure and Psychic Change*. Madison, CT: International Universities Press.

Hurn, H.T. (1971) 'Toward a paradigm of the terminal phase: the current status of the terminal phase'. *Journal of the American Psychoanalytic Association*, 19: 332–348.

Jacobson, E. (1954) 'Transference problems in the psychoanalytic treatment of severely depressive patients'. *Journal of the American Psychoanalytic Association*, 2: 595–606.

—— (1964) *The Self and the Object World*. New York: International Universities Press.

Jahoda, M. (1958) *Current Concepts of Positive Mental Health*. New York: Basic Books.

Johan, M. (1989) (reporter) 'Evaluation of outcome of psychoanalytic treatment: should followup by the analyst be part of the post-termination phase of analytic treatment?' *Journal of the American Psychoanalytic Association*, 37: 813–822.

Jones, E. (1913) 'The attitude of the psychoanalytic physician towards current conflicts'. In: *Papers on Psychoanalysis*, 2nd edn. London: Baillière, Tindall & Cox, 1918, pp. 312–317.

—— (1931) 'The concept of a normal mind'. In: S.D. Schmalhausen (ed.), *The Neurotic Age*. New York: Ferrar & Rinehart, pp. 65–81.

—— (1936) 'The criteria of success in treatment'. In: *Papers on Psychoanalysis*, 5th edn. London: Baillière, Tindall & Cox, 1948, pp. 379–383.

—— (1942) 'The concept of a normal mind'. *International Journal of Psycho-Analysis*, 23: 1–8.

—— (1953–57) *The Life and Work of Sigmund Freud*, 3 volumes. New York: Basic Books.

Kantrowitz, J.L., Katz, N.L., Greenman, D.A., Morris, H., Paolitto, F., Sashin, J. and Solomon, L. (1989) 'The patient–analyst match and the outcome of psychoanalysis: a pilot study'. *Journal of the American Psychoanalytic Association*, 37: 893–919.

Kelman, H. (1956) (reporter) Panel: 'Goals in therapy'. *The American Journal of Psychoanalysis*, 16: 3–23.

Kernberg, O. (1975) *Borderline Conditions and Pathological Narcissism*. New York: Jason Aronson.

—— (1984) *Severe Personality Disorders: Psychotherapeutic Strategies*. New Haven: Yale University Press.

Khan, M., Davis, J.A. and Davis, M.E.V. (1974) 'The beginnings and fruition of the self'. In: J.A. Davis and J. Dobbing (eds) *Scientific Foundations of Paediatrics*. London: W. Heinemann, pp. 626–640.

King, P. and Steiner, R. (1991) *The Freud–Klein Controversies 1941–45*. London: Routledge.

Klein, M. (1946) 'Notes on some schizoid mechanisms'. In: M. Klein, P. Heimann, S. Isaacs and J. Riviere (eds) *Developments in Psycho-Analysis*. London: Hogarth Press, 1952, pp. 292–320.

—— (1950) 'On the criteria for the termination of an analysis'. *International Journal of Psycho-Analysis*, 31: 204.

—— (1975) *Envy and Gratitude and Other Works 1946–63*. London: Hogarth Press.

Knight, R.P. (1942) 'Evaluation of the results of psychoanalytic therapy'. *American Journal of Psychiatry*, 98: 434–446.

Kohut, H. (1971) *The Analysis of the Self*. New York: International Universities Press.

—— (1984) *How Does Analysis Cure?* Chicago: University of Chicago Press.

Kramer, M.K. (1959) 'On continuation of the analytic process after psychoanalysis (a self-observation)'. *International Journal of Psycho-Analysis*, 40: 17–25.

Kramer, S. and Akhtar, S. (1988) 'The developmental context of preoedipal object relations: clinical application of Mahler's theory of symbiosis and separation–individuation'. *Psychoanalytic Quarterly*, 57: 547–576.

Krapf, E.E. (1961) 'The concepts of normality and mental health in psycho-analysis'. *International Journal of Psycho-Analysis*, 42: 439–446.

Kris, E. (1956) 'On some vicissitudes of insight in psychoanalysis'. *International Journal of Psycho-Analysis*, 37: 445–455.

Lampl-de Groot, J. (1957) 'On defense and development: normal and patho-logical'. *Psychoanalytic Study of the Child*, 12: 114–126.

Lichtenberg, J.D. (1983) *Psychoanalysis and Infant Research*. Hillsdale, NJ: Analytic Press.

Little, M. (1958) 'On delusional transference (transference psychosis)'. *International Journal of Psycho-Analysis*, 39: 134–138.

Loewald, H.W. (1960) 'On the therapeutic action of psychoanalysis'. In: *Papers on Psychoanalysis*. New Haven: Yale University Press, 1980, pp. 221–256.

—— (1970) 'Psychoanalytic theory and the psychoanalytic process'. In: *Papers on Psychoanalysis:* New Haven: Yale University Press, 1980, pp. 277–301.

—— (1981) 'Regression: some general considerations'. *Psychoanalytic Quarterly*, 50: 22–43.

Luborsky, L., Krits-Christoph, R., Mintz, J. and Auerbach, A. (1988) *Who Will Benefit from Psychotherapy? Predicting Therapeutic Outcomes*. New York: Basic Books.

Mahler, M. (1968) *On Human Symbiosis and the Vicissitudes of Individuation*, vol. I, *Infantile Psychosis*. New York: International Universities Press.

——, Pine, F. and Bergman, A. (1975) *The Psychological Birth of the Human Infant*. New York: Basic Books.

Martin, G.C. (1993) (reporter) Panel: 'Stability of gains achieved during analytic treatment from a followup perspective'. *Journal of the American Psychoanalytic*

Association, 41: 209–217.

McGlashan, T.H. and Miller, G.H. (1982) 'The goals of psychoanalysis and psychoanalytic psychotherapy'. *Archives of General Psychiatry*, 39: 377–388.

McNutt, E.R. (1992) (reporter) Panel: 'Psychoanalysis and psychoanalytic psychotherapy – similarities and differences: indications, contraindications, and initiation'. *Journal of the American Psychoanalytic Association*, 40: 223–238.

Meissner, W. (1991) 'A decade of psychoanalytic praxis'. *Psychoanalytic Inquiry*, 11: 30–64.

Menninger, K.A. (1958) *Theory of Psychoanalytic Technique*. London: Imago.

Milner, M. (1950) 'Short communications: a note on the ending of an analysis'. *International Journal of Psycho-Analysis*, 31: 191–193.

Mitchell, S.A. (1988) *Relational Concepts in Psychoanalysis: An Integration*. Cambridge, MA: Harvard University Press.

Modell, A. (1976) ' "The holding environment" and the therapeutic action of psychoanalysis'. *Journal of the American Psychoanalytic Association*, 24: 284–307.

Moore, B.E. and Fine, B.D. (1990) *Psychoanalytic Terms and Concepts*. New Haven and London: American Psychoanalytic Association and Yale University Press.

Morgenstern, S.A. (1976) (reporter) Panel: 'Current concepts of the psycho-analytic process'. *Journal of the American Psychoanalytic Association*, 24: 181–195.

Morgenthaler, F. (1978) *Technik. Zur Dialektik der psychoanalytischen Praxis*. Frankfurt am Main: Syndikat.

Morris, J.L. (1992) (reporter) Panel: 'Psychoanalysis and psychoanalytic psycho-therapy – similarities and differences: therapeutic technique'. *Journal of the American Psychoanalytic Association*, 40: 211–221.

Murphy, G. (1975) *Outgrowing Self-Deception*. New York: Basic Books.

Naiman, J. (1976) (reporter) Panel: 'The fundamentals of psychic change in clinical practice'. *International Journal of Psycho-Analysis*, 57: 411–418.

Nersessian, E. (1989) (reporter) Panel: 'Changing psychic structure through treatment'. *Journal of the American Psychoanalytic Association*, 37: 173–185.

Nunberg, H. (1928) 'Problems of therapy'. In: *Practice and Theory of Psychoanalysis*. New York: International Universities Press, 1948.

—— (1937) 'Symposium on the theory of the therapeutic results of psychoanalysis'. *International Journal of Psycho-Analysis*, 18: 161–169.

Oberndorf, C.P. (1948) 'Results of psychoanalytic therapy'. *International Journal of Psycho-Analysis*, 29: 107–114.

—— (1950) 'Unsatisfactory results of psychoanalytic therapy'. *Psychoanalytic Quarterly*, 19: 393–407.

——, Greenacre, P. and Kubie, L. (1948) 'Symposium on the evaluation of thera-peutic results'. *International Journal of Psycho-Analysis*, 29: 7–33.

Orr, D.W. (1954) 'Transference and countertransference: a historical survey'. *Journal of the American Psychoanalytic Association*, 2: 621–669.

Payne, S. (1950) 'Short communication on criteria for terminating analysis'. *International Journal of Psycho-Analysis*, 31: 205.

Pfeffer, A.Z. (1961) 'Follow-up study of a satisfactory analysis'. *Journal of the*

American Psychoanalytic Association, 9: 698–718.

—— (1963a) (reporter) Panel: 'Analysis terminable and interminable – twenty-five years later'. *Journal of the American Psychoanalytic Association*, 11: 131–142.

—— (1963b) 'The meaning of the analyst after analysis: a contribution to the theory of therapeutic results'. *Journal of the American Psychoanalytic Association*, 11: 224–244.

—— (1993) 'After the analysis: analyst as both old and new object'. *Journal of the American Psychoanalytic Association*, 41: 323–337.

Pulver S.E. (1991) 'Psychoanalytic technique: progress during the past decade'. *Psychoanalytic Inquiry*, 11: 65–87.

—— (1993) 'The eclectic analyst, or the many roads to insight and change'. *Journal of the American Psychoanalytic Association*, 41: 339–357.

Rado, S. (1925) 'The economic principle in psychoanalytic technique'. *International Journal of Psycho-Analysis*, 6: 35–44.

Rangell, L. (1954) 'Similarities and differences between psychoanalysis and dynamic psychotherapy'. *Journal of the American Psychoanalytic Association*, 2: 734–744.

—— (1987) 'A core process in psychoanalytic treatment'. *Psychoanalytic Quarterly*, 56: 240–249.

Rank, O. (1924) *The Trauma of Birth*. London: Routledge & Kegan Paul.

Rapaport, D. (1951) *Organization and Pathology of Thought*. New York: Columbia University Press.

—— (1958) 'The theory of ego autonomy: a generalisation'. *Bulletin of the Menninger Clinic*, 22: 13–35.

Reich, W. (1924a) Remarks summarized in: *Bulletin of the IPA*. *International Journal of Psycho-Analysis*, 5: 391–408.

—— (1924b) 'Über Genitalität'. *Zeitschrift für Psychoanalyse*, X: 164–179.

—— (1928) 'Indications and dangers of character-analysis'. In: *Character Analysis*. London: Vision Press, 3rd edn, 1950, pp. 114–118.

Rickman, J. (1950) 'On the criteria for the termination of an analysis'. *International Journal of Psycho-Analysis*, 31: 200–201.

Riesman, D., Glazer, N. and Denney, R. (1950) *The Lonely Crowd*. New Haven: Yale University Press.

Robbins, B.S. (1960) 'The process of cure in psychotherapy'. In: P.H. Hoch and J. Zubin (eds) *Current Approaches to Psychoanalysis*. New York and London: Grune & Stratton, pp. 96–108.

Robbins, W.S. (1975) (reporter) Panel: 'Termination: problems and techniques'. *Journal of the American Psychoanalytic Association*, 23: 166–176.

Rosenfeld, H. (1954) 'Considerations regarding the psychoanalytic approach to acute and chronic schizophrenia in psychotic states'. In: *Psychotic States*. London: Hogarth Press, 1965, pp. 117–127.

Sachs, H. (1925) 'Metapsychological points of view in technique and theory'. *International Journal of Psycho-Analysis*, 6: 5–12.

Sander, L. (1975) 'Infant and caretaking environment: investigation and conceptualization of adaptive behaviours in a series of increasing complexity'. In: E.J.

Anthony (ed.) *Explorations in Child Psychiatry*. New York: Plenum, pp. 129–166.

Sandler, J. (1974) 'Psychological conflict and the structural model: some clinical and theoretical implications'. *International Journal of Psycho-Analysis*, 55: 53–62.

—— (1983) 'Reflections on some relations between psychoanalytic concepts and psychoanalytic practice'. *International Journal of Psycho-Analysis*, 64: 35–45.

—— (ed.) (1987) *Projection, Identification, Projective Identification*. Madison, CT: International Universities Press.

—— (1988) 'Psychoanalytic treatment and "Analysis terminable and interminable" '. *International Journal of Psycho-Analysis*, 69: 335–345.

—— (ed.) (1991) *On Freud's 'Analysis Terminable and Interminable'*. New Haven: Yale University Press.

—— and Joffe, W.G. (1967) 'On the psychoanalytic theory of autonomy and the autonomy of psychoanalytic theory'. *International Journal of Psychiatry*, 3: 512–515.

—— and Sandler, A.-M. (1983) 'The "second censorship", the "three box model", and some technical implications'. *International Journal of Psycho-Analysis*, 64: 413–425.

—— and Freud, A. (1985) *The Analysis of Defense: The Ego and the Mechanisms of Defense Revisited*. Madison, CT: International Universities Press.

——, Holder, A. and Meers, D. (1963) 'The ego ideal and the ideal self'. *The Psychoanalytic Study of the Child*, 18: 139–158.

——, Dreher, A.U. and Drews, S. (1991) 'An approach to conceptual research in psychoanalysis illustrated by the consideration of psychic trauma'. *International Review of Psychoanalysis*, 18: 133–141.

——, Dare, C. and Holder, A. (1992) *The Patient and the Analyst*, 2nd edn. Madison, CT: International Universities Press.

——, Dreher, A.U., Drews, S., Fischer, R., Klüwer, R., Muck, M., Vogel, H. and Will, C. (1987) *Psychisches Trauma: Ein Konzept im Theorie-Praxis-Zusammenhang*. Frankfurt am Main: Materialien aus dem Sigmund-Freud-Institut Frankfurt, 5.

Schachter, J. (1994) 'Abstinence and neutrality: development and diverse views'. *International Journal of Psycho-Analysis*, 75: 709–721.

Schafer, R. (1994) 'The practice of revisiting classics: an essay on Heinz Hartmann's *Psychoanalysis and Moral Values*'. *Psychoanalysis and Contemporary Thought*, 17: 251–285.

Schlessinger, N. and Robbins, F. (1974) 'Assessment and follow-up in psychoanalysis'. *Journal of the American Psychoanalytic Association*, 22: 542–567.

Schuker, E. (1990) (reporter) Panel: 'Effects of theory on psychoanalytic technique and on the development of psychoanalytic process'. *Journal of the American Psychoanalytic Association*, 38: 221–233.

Segal, H. (1950) 'Some aspects of the analysis of a schizophrenic'. *International Journal of Psycho-Analysis*, 31: 268–278.

Shaw, R.R. (1991) (reporter) Panel: 'Concepts and controversies about the transference neurosis'. *Journal of the American Psychoanalytic Association*, 39: 227–239.

Spillius, E.B. (ed.) (1988a) *Melanie Klein Today: Developments in Theory and Practice*, vol. I, *Mainly Theory*. London: Routledge.

—— (1988b) *Melanie Klein Today: Developments in Theory and Practice*, vol. II, *Mainly Practice*. London: Routledge.

Spitz, R.A. (1957) *No and Yes: On the Genesis of Human Communication*. New York: International Universities Press.

—— (1965) *The First Year of Life*. New York: International Universities Press.

Steiner, J. (1989) 'The aim of psychoanalysis'. *Psychoanalytic Psychotherapy*, 4: 109–120.

Steiner, R. (1994) 'Some observations on the role of extra-analytical variables in the theoretical and clinical issues of the Freud–Klein controversial discussions (1941–1944) and their relevance today'. *Bulletin of the British Psycho-Analytical Society*, 30, 7: 2–33.

Stern, D.N. (1977) *The First Relationship: Infant and Mother*. Cambridge, MA: Harvard University Press.

—— (1985) *The Interpersonal World of the Infant*. New York: Basic Books.

Stone, L. (1954) 'The widening scope of indications for psychoanalysis'. *Journal of the American Psychoanalytic Association*, 2: 567–594.

—— (1961) *The Psychoanalytic Situation*. New York: International Universities Press.

—— (1982) 'The influence of the practice and theory of psychotherapy on education in psychoanalysis'. In: E.D. Joseph and R.S. Wallerstein (eds) *Psychotherapy: Impact on Psychoanalytic Training*. New York: International Universities Press, pp. 75–118.

Strachey, J. (1934) 'The nature of the therapeutic action of psychoanalysis'. *International Journal of Psycho-Analysis*, 15: 127–159.

—— (1937) 'Symposium on the theory of the therapeutic results of psychoanalysis'. *International Journal of Psycho-Analysis*, 18: 139–145.

Sulloway, F.J. (1979) *Freud, Biologist of the Mind. Beyond the Psychoanalytic Legend*. London: Burnett Books.

Szasz, T.S. (1957) 'On the theory of psychoanalytic treatment'. *International Journal of Psycho-Analysis*, 38: 166–182.

Ticho, E.A. (1971) 'Probleme des Abschlusses der psychoanalytischen Therapie'. *Psyche*, 25: 44–56.

—— (1972) 'Termination of psychoanalysis: treatment goals, life goals'. *Psychoanalytic Quarterly*, 41: 315–333.

Ticho, G.R. (1967) 'On self-analysis'. *International Journal of Psycho-Analysis*, 48: 308–318.

Viederman, M. (1991) 'The real person of the analyst and his role in the process of psychoanalytic cure'. *Journal of the American Psychoanalytic Association*, 39: 451–490.

Waelder, R. (1936) 'The problem of freedom in psychoanalysis and the problem of reality-testing'. *International Journal of Psycho-Analysis*, 17: 89–108.

—— (1960) *Basic Theory of Psychoanalysis*. New York: International Universities Press.

Wallerstein, R.S. (1965) 'The goals of psychoanalysis: a survey of analytic view-points'. *Journal of the American Psychoanalytic Association*, 13: 748–770.

—— (1986) *Forty-two Lives in Treatment: A Study of Psychoanalysis and Psychotherapy.* New York: Guilford Press.

—— (1988) 'One psychoanalysis or many?' *International Journal of Psycho-Analysis*, 69: 5–21.

—— (1992) 'The goals of psychoanalysis reconsidered'. In: A. Sugarman, R. Nemiroff and D. Greenson (eds) *The Technique and Practice of Psychoanalysis*, vol. II. Madison, CT: International Universities Press, pp. 63–90.

—— (1995) *'The Talking Cure': The Psychoanalyses and the Psychotherapies.* New Haven: Yale University Press.

Weigert, E. (1954) 'The importance of flexibility in psychoanalytic technique'. *Journal of the American Psychoanalytic Association*, 2: 702–710.

Weinshel, E.M. (1990) 'How wide is the widening scope of psychoanalysis and how solid is its structural model? Some concerns and observations'. *Journal of the American Psychoanalytic Association*, 38: 272–296.

—— and Renik, O. (1991) 'The past ten years: psychoanalysis in the United States, 1980–1990'. *Psychoanalytic Inquiry*, 11: 13–29.

Winnicott, D.W. (1954) 'Withdrawal and regression'. In: *Collected Papers.* London: Tavistock, 1958.

—— (1960a) 'The theory of the parent–infant relationship'. In: *The Maturational Processes and the Facilitating Environment.* London: Hogarth Press, 1976, pp. 37–55.

—— (1960b) 'Ego distortion in terms of true and false self'. In: *The Maturational Processes and the Facilitating Environment.* London: Hogarth Press, 1976, pp. 140–152.

—— (1962) 'The aims of psychoanalytical treatment'. In: *The Maturational Processes and the Facilitating Environment.* London: Hogarth Press, 1976, pp. 166–170.

Zetzel, E. (1965) 'The theory of therapy in relation to a developmental model of the psychic apparatus'. *International Journal of Psycho-Analysis*, 46: 39–52.

Name index

Ackerman, N. 61
Alexander, F. 24, 25, 60, 71;
    superego 26–8, 33
Altman, L.L. 79
Arlow, J. 93, 106–7

Bader, M. 101
Balint, M. 8, 46, 64, 104; genital
    primacy 54; new beginning 37–8,
    54
Barchilon, J. 58
Bergler, E. 35–6
Bibring, E. 35, 36–7, 60
Bion, W. 4
Brenner, C. 107
Buxbaum, E. 56

Chessick, R. 5
Cooper, A.M. 2, 84, 101, 102, 103;
    pluralism and integration 109;
    psychotherapy and psychoanalysis
    111–12
Cramer, B. 93–4

Deutsch, H. 80
Diethelm, O. 61

Eissler, K.R. 58, 69, 83–4, 92
Etchegoyen, R.H. 99

Fairbairn, R. 63, 66–8, 70, 90, 104
Fenichel, O. 23–4, 28, 35, 47–8
Ferenczi, S. 24, 29–31

Fine, B.D. 4–5, 57, 85
Firestein, S.K. 80
Flournoy, O. 93–4
Freud, A. 20, 31, 46, 76, 107; analytic
    technique 60; British Society 52;
    defence mechanisms 38–9; and
    topographical theory 33
Freud, S. 1, 10–22, 23, 33, 45–6, 52,
    107, 116; analysis and therapy
    11–13, 18–19, 22, 114; morality 4;
    'structural' theory 6–7, 18–21,
    24–5, 32; 'topographical' theory 6,
    10–11
Fromm-Reichmann, F. 60
Furst, S. 97–8

Gaskill, H. 98
Gill, M.M. 60
Gitelson, M. 61, 78, 79
Glover, E. 35, 63–4
Glueck, B. 73–5
Goldberg, A. 103
Greenacre, P. 51
Greenson, R. 71, 90
Grinberg, L. 98–9
Grotjahn, M. 80

Hartmann, H. 7, 31, 38, 46, 84;
    adaptation 40–1, 44–5; autonomy
    78; ego psychology 39–41, 57, 83;
    mental health 42–5, 68; rationality
    75
Hoffer, W. 53–4, 80

Subject index

adaptation 40–1, 44–5; flexible 76; social 93
aims 5–6; framework for 113–23
alloplastic adaptation 40
American Psychiatric Association 61
American Psychoanalytic Association 58, 60, 62, 72, 83, 90, 91; Committee on the Evaluation of Psychoanalytic Therapy 58–9; psychoanalytic psychotherapy 109–10
analysis process 119–21
analyst–patient interaction 103–4, 121; empathy 103; Fairbairn 67–8; termination 89–90; Ticho 87–9; value systems 118
anxiety 23; persecutory and depressive anxieties 53
attainable goals 72–3
autonomy 78; ego functions 40
autoplastic adaptation 40

baby-watchers 107
balance 75–6; psychic 42
bedrock 107
Berlin Institute 7, 50
birth, trauma of 20
blinkers 5
borderline personality disorder 83, 86
Boston Psychoanalytic Society 7, 50–1
British Psychoanalytical Society 7, 105; groups within 52–4, 63–4, 71–2

censorship 3
character change 28–9
character traits 37
child analysis 62, 76
child development *see* development
'classical' psychoanalysis 8, 83, 98
clinical issues 97–101
clinical and technical perspective 9, 119
'common ground' 100
completion 80–1; *see also* termination
conflict 107, 115; Alexander 26; Fenichel 47–8; Freud 13–14, 15, 16–17; Hartmann 44–5
'conjunction' statement 11
Contemporary Freudians 52
corrective emotional experience 71
cost-effectiveness 119
countertransference 4, 118
countertransference cures 58
cure *see* therapy

death instinct 22, 104
defences: child analysis 62; Fenichel 47–8; A. Freud 38–9; S. Freud 13–14
depression 43, 59
depressive anxieties 53
development 119; balance 75–6; defects 107–8; ego 70–1; A. Freud 52; interruption of 88–9; Klein 52; separation-individuation 91; therapeutic process and 78–9, 79